PLANNING
FLEXIBLE LEARNING
PLACES

..

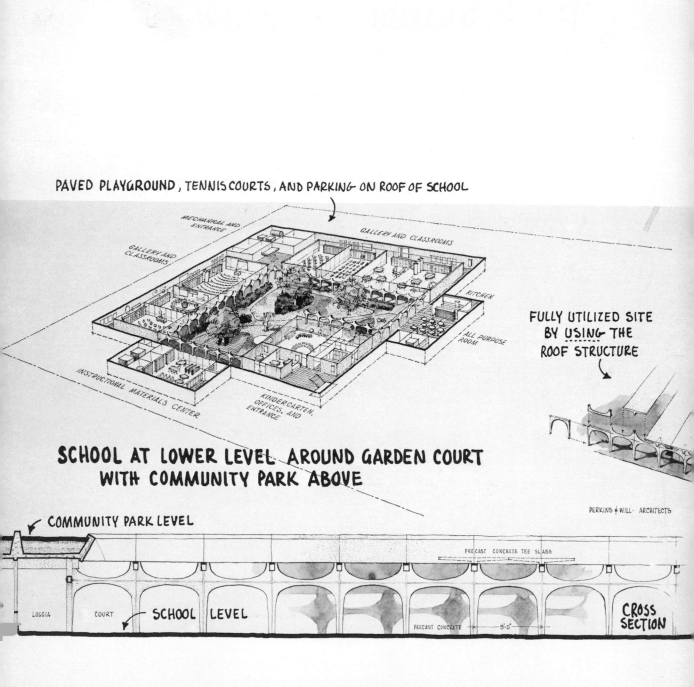

PAVED PLAYGROUND, TENNIS COURTS, AND PARKING ON ROOF OF SCHOOL

MECHANICAL AND ENTRANCE

GALLERY AND CLASSROOMS

GALLERY AND CLASSROOMS

KITCHEN

ALL PURPOSE ROOM

FULLY UTILIZED SITE BY USING THE ROOF STRUCTURE

INSTRUCTIONAL MATERIALS CENTER

KINDERGARTEN, OFFICES, AND ENTRANCE

SCHOOL AT LOWER LEVEL AROUND GARDEN COURT WITH COMMUNITY PARK ABOVE

PERKINS & WILL ARCHITECTS

COMMUNITY PARK LEVEL

PRECAST CONCRETE TEE SLABS

LOGGIA   COURT   SCHOOL LEVEL

PRECAST CONCRETE   9'-0"

CROSS SECTION

PLANNING FLEXIBLE LEARNING PLACES

..

STANTON LEGGETT
Stanton Leggett and Associates, Inc.
Educational Consultants
Martha's Vineyard, Mass., and Chicago

C. WILLIAM BRUBAKER
Perkins & Will Architects
Chicago

AARON COHODES
Teach 'em, Inc.
Chicago

ARTHUR S. SHAPIRO
George Peabody College
Nashville

..

McGRAW-HILL BOOK COMPANY

New York St. Louis San Francisco Auckland Bogotá Düsseldorf
Johannesburg London Madrid Mexico Montreal
New Delhi Panama Paris São Paulo Singapore
Sydney Tokyo Toronto

Library of Congress Cataloging in Publication Data

Main entry under title:
    Planning flexible learning places.

    Includes index.
    1. School facilities—Planning.   2. Schools—
Furniture, equipment, etc. I. Leggett, Stanton F.

LB3221.P58   371.6′2   76-46927
ISBN 0-07-037060-5

1234567890   KPKP   786543210987

The editors for this book were Jeremy Robinson and Tobia L. Worth,
the designer was Edward J. Fox, and the production supervisor
was Frank P. Bellantoni. It was set in Souvenir
by University Graphics, Inc.

Printed and bound by The Kingsport Press.

CONTENTS

PREFACE

■ ■ The purpose of this book is not to win converts to new concepts, although that's not a bad target. A better one, though, is to provide some useful design and curriculum options that school districts can adopt, for the most part with the budgets and teacher staffs they now have.

Anyone with a speculative nature could design a new public school system from scratch. It might even work better than the one we now have. But the one we have is not going to disappear. What we need are ways to build on what is available.

This book is planned to help those concerned with developing new school facilities or with remodeling or changing existing facilities. As such, it is directed toward school administrators and board members and to their partners in planning: teachers, architects, students, planners, and community leaders. The emphasis is on flexibility, defined in *Webster's New International Dictionary* (second edition) as " . . . adaptability; as, the *flexibility* of whalebone, rays of light, a person's mind, a course of study."

Thus, there are two aspects of flexibility. One is the technically marvelous ability of properly designed building space to respond to new uses. In this sense, the new enclosure for education is a tool for teaching, responsive often far beyond the demands made upon it. The other aspect of flexibility lies in the changing requirements that developments in education make upon space. Here the going is much tougher. The interactions of educational programs with space response have been illustrated by a variety of models in the education of young children, in the preadolescent period, and in adolescent times—all under widely differing circumstances.

Ideally, the real-world school is a series of readjustments between the environment of the building and educational programs either at work or in the process of course correction, redefinition, and improvement. The design of a school facility is a continuing process in which the walls, the expanse of space, the many kinds of equipment, and the educational program form the palette and the designers are teachers, students, parents, custodians, school administrators, school board members, and architects. The design task is never completed.

A smaller goal of this book is to help school people and school boards adjust to the challenge of change. Change is rarely a comfortable process. This is especially true in education, in which results are hard to measure and take a long time to compute. It is a lamentable fact that the returns won't be in on the products of current educational practices until it is too late to make any meaningful adjustments. When the performance of this generation can be appraised with certainty, the students will no longer be students but the parents of students, and the cycle will be ready to start again.

The trouble with the worst-looking school you've ever seen is that it won't be a disaster for all children. If it were, we might tear it down faster. But bright kids and kids with zest have so many things going for them that the shape of the building, the size of the classroom, the quality of the instructional materials, and even a mediocre teacher won't hold them back. A few children will learn what they have to know in spite of the emotional and intellectual hurdles that parents and teachers and administrators and school boards erect without even trying.

But the rest of the nation's students—the great majority—must be helped to try harder than they know how to try, to reach higher than they know how to reach, and to think better than they know how to think. This book has these goals in mind. It is also planned to help school boards and administrators take an informed look at what's ahead for education. The danger to guard against is that we might decide as a nation to fight the battles of the 1960s all over again and build the schools of the 1960s all over again.

We hope not.

No one can be proud of the bickering and fuss that accompanied education in the last decade. Certainly board members have good reason for being dismayed when they recall their response to some issues. Long hair, short skirts, pot, beards, four-letter words, protests over everything—these are the lamentable hallmarks of education in the sixties. When such issues arise, as they must, and when they wind up in the courts, as they frequently do, nobody looks good, not even the winners.

A lot of people lent a hand with the ideas in this book. Much of the conceptual material interpreted by us in formulating proposals for the education of young children came from the brilliant work of Benjamin Bloom. We have all learned much from his insights into the educational process. Frank Lassiter, when he was with Stanton Leggett and Associates, made major contributions to the understanding of the dynamics of the interaction between equipment and learning. Portions of the book appeared in various issues of *Nation's Schools,* a McGraw-Hill magazine for school administrators that is no longer published. The section on forecasting school enrollments appeared in modified form in *The American School Board Journal* (January 1973).

Finally, we don't expect everyone to applaud all our suggestions or, indeed, to try them all. We do hope, though, that they will be considered with the problems of the 1970s, not the 1960s or the 1950s, in mind.

The thing to remember about the old days is not that they were good or bad but that they are no longer around.

THE AUTHORS

CHAPTER 1

THE FIRST TWELVE YEARS: SCHOOL AND HOME REINFORCE LEARNING

■ ■ DIFFERENCES APPEAR AMONG children in the earliest days of school as they approach a new task of school learning. Most teachers, facing children at the start of a school year, expect these differences. They anticipate that perhaps one-third will learn well, one-third will learn something, and one-third will not learn the materials with which the teacher expects the class to deal. Most teachers are reconciled to this kind of performance, and they get it. Worse yet, schools also teach children to be reconciled to these apparently insurmountable differences. In most schools, the divergence grows between good learner and poor learner the longer the children are in school.

Yet an increasing amount of research denies this almost-Calvinistic notion of predetermined learning ability. This research suggests that individuals differ with respect to school learning most significantly in the rate of speed of learning. If the schools manage learning properly, the differences in the rate of speed of learning can be markedly reduced and under ideal conditions may even approach zero. Schools, as they now operate, may actually cause individual differences in school learning where research shows it is possible to reduce or even to eliminate those differences.

We are so well accustomed to our biases that it is hard to imagine schools in which virtually all students master the school learning that is required. Even in highly selective private schools, teachers seem to have the same expectations of a normal distribution of students in terms of success or failure in learning. Yet in a normal distribution of the school population, excluding perhaps 10 to 15 percent of the students who have disabilities in one form or another for the subject or for school learning, 90 to 85 percent of the students may be expected under favorable conditions to reach a level of mastery of a topic or a subject equivalent to, say, an A grade. The major condition is that an appropriate amount of time be available to each student. Now we organize most instruction as if all children learned at the same rate of speed.

Using a mastery learning approach, the school helps a student understand what he should learn by making clear to him what he is expected to learn. Mastery learning also helps the student diagnose what he does not yet know. Given this diagnostic information, the student takes the time he needs to master what he does not yet know. Some students, obviously, will move much faster than others through parts of the curriculum. Students who require a longer period of time will be supported by special materials and by additional help and encouragement. This process matches the learning procedures to the learning styles of the student. Some practices that help in this approach are small group sessions in which students assist each other, tutoring, and a broader selection of appropriate learning materials. The assumption behind this program is that the student can and will learn if suitable help is given.

Observation suggests that at the outset of a series of learning tasks the difference in the speed of learning of the fast as against the slow students in a class may be at the level of 5 to 1 as measured in elapsed time. At the end of a series of interrelated learning tasks, the difference in elapsed time should decrease to approximately 3 to 1.

If time spent on the task is considered, highly significant implications for the learning process are apparent. Bloom[1] reports that at the beginning of a series of learning tasks children under mastery learning procedures and children under traditional procedures both spent about 65 percent of the classroom time working on the task. By the final task, mastery students had increased the amount of time spent on the task to 85 percent, whereas nonmastery students, including those who had become incapable of dealing effectively with the material, were spending about 50 percent of the time on the task, a decline from their starting level.

When on-task time is considered, in the early learning tasks of a sequence using mastery strategy the difference in the rate of speed of learning is about 3 to 1. At the end

---

[1] Benjamin S. Bloom, "Time and Learning," Thorndike Award Address, Eighty-first Annual Convention of the American Psychological Association, Montreal, August 27, 1973.

of the sequence the time spent on the task is about 1 to 1.5 or less. As Bloom states, "Students become more efficient in their learning under favorable learning conditions and . . .students become more and more alike in their learning efficiency as measured by time devoted directly to the learning process."[2]

VERBAL EDUCATION AND THE INFLUENCE OF THE HOME

It is clear that reading comprehension and knowledge of words are critical skills when a very large percentage of learning is gained through listening to the teachers' explanations or instruction and reading instructional materials. Studies in the United States and in other countries reported by the International Project for the Evaluation of Educational Achievement (IEA) show that a good deal of ability in these verbal areas is influenced more strongly by the home than by the school. The schools can deal with the differences developed before school entrance by providing verbal education in the school, especially in the ages from six to ten.[3]

Cooperation between home and school is most important in improving the development of preschool verbal ability. The ways in which parents and nursery school and parents and primary school work together are most significant. In the primary school the research suggests:

> . . . specific instruction in the particular features of language, thought, and reading on which these children appear to be most deficient. Many of the curricula require special techniques of patterned practice in the classrooms, a great deal of success on the part of children supplemented by frequent and varied rewards and reinforcements, and appropriate classroom evaluation and corrective procedures to insure each part of the learning process.[4]

FACILITIES INTERPRETATIONS

As Bloom[5] points out in looking at the implications of the IEA studies, the use of strategies such as mastery learning that are closely related to existing educational conditions offer significant opportunities for improvement in the quality of instruction at lower cost and in shorter time

---

[2]Ibid., p. 20.

[3]Benjamin A. Bloom, "Implications of the IEA Studies for Curriculum and Instruction," *The School Review,* University of Chicago, May 1974, p. 423.

[4]Ibid., p. 424.

[5]Ibid., p. 434.

than do global reforms of education or changes accomplished through the training and retraining of teachers.

A model of elementary education

- Probably should start with three-year-olds and go at least to age ten or eleven or about the fifth or sixth grade. This observation relates tangentially to Jean Piaget's views on the importance of a relatively stable learning environment through these years.
- Should have vastly increased and much more significant opportunities for parents and the school to work together in and out of school to reduce differences among children in their ability to deal with school learning.
- Should measure itself on such factors as time spent on the learning task, reduction of time necessary to learn segments of material to mastery, and similar measures that relate to the potential of reducing individual differences among students in the rate of speed of learning to mastery.
- Could include a core of education related to discovery in science, the development of skills in social studies, the arts, and physical education that only later may be included in the concentration on mastery education.
- Could be constructed so that the effect of the "latent" curriculum as well as the overt or manifest curriculum is utilized. The manifest curriculum is the direct process of instruction. The latent curriculum is the cumulative effect of the way the school is organized, what its acted-out values are, what the relationship between teachers and students is, and how this affects life in the schools. The traditional school in its latent curriculum taught very clearly conformity to correct behavioral patterns, neatness, promptness, law and order, and the like.

A model of elementary education, using the strategy of learning to mastery, must accommodate individual differences in the rate of speed of learning, must provide for feedback and corrective measures, and must furnish increasingly appropriate learning materials that are closely matched to the learning style of the student. To focus on what is most readily possible, the school may use certain specific skill areas like reading, language arts, and mathematics at the elementary school level for emphasis in its mastery program. As this approach includes helping students with deficiencies in verbal education, the possibility of significant change is strengthened.

By the way they operate some schools teach students

that doing one's own thing is most important, that students thrive on disorder, and that expressing one's self is a major function. The school with a mastery learning strategy, with its high concern for reducing individual differences in the speed of learning, finds in the use of time on the task a highly significant index of success in learning. The latent curriculum must support this value of the school. On the other hand, it is possible in the core areas to focus more intensively on interaction among students, creative thinking, and the mind-stretching functions involved in problem solving and allied aspects of learning.

SIZE OF THE SCHOOL

The major research findings suggest with increasing emphasis, and the IEA studies in education in particular point to, the universality of the power of the home in the area of verbal learning. This point is singled out because schools institutionalize verbal learning, or the ability to learn from reading and understanding oral instruction. If the schools are constrained in the performance of their task by the learning conditions provided in the home, then the school either acts to help change those conditions or moves its program so as to rely less strongly upon verbal education.

The Head Start program moved in the direction of supplementing the home but lacked real integration with the school. "Sesame Street" and similar television programs are designed to have a supportive impact on home education. The home-school centers of the Chicago Board of Education, by enlisting the close cooperation of parents, had substantial success in school units that ranged from groups of three- and four-year-olds to approximately the second grade.

This background suggests a number of characteristics of the school, one of which is that the size of the school should be a function of the number of preschool and school-age children's parents that can become involved with the school in a sufficiently close pattern. On this basis, the number of parents may be stated with respect to children from birth to eleven years of age. If there were 25 children per year, the spectrum would involve a total of 300 children with perhaps 200 to 250 sets of parents. This group of 400 to 500 parents would probably represent as large a group as could be dealt with in a small school in which the school setting would be designed to influence the ways parents educated their children.

The school would then be embracing a twofold educational mission: helping children learn and cooperating with parents so that they would learn to be better teachers of their children. This concept moves far beyond the usual PTA, which is attended largely by parents who are already good teachers of their children, and means that the school must reach out to those who need assistance in teaching and who often are aware of the need but have no means of help available.

THE SCHOOLS AND THE WORKING MOTHER

There is an increasing trend toward families in which both parents work even when children are quite young. The revolution in the role of women and inflation pressures will no doubt accelerate this trend. Probably in time in the cities 80 to 90 percent of the mothers of elementary school children will work. Accordingly, the notion of child care centers as an occasional need is changing to the requirement for care of children from the time that they come to school in the morning, which would precede the mothers' leaving for work, to the time that mothers can pick up children from school–child care provision after work.

One effective way to provide care for children who are very young is home care, in which a parent maintains a program for three or four children in addition to the parent's own (see Fig. 1-1). If forty children out of seventy-five in ages up to two years required home care services, the parents operating these units could well become strong allies of the school. Ten or twelve parents operating home care centers might require service from the school that would allow it to help improve the setting for learning at early ages. This service could significantly affect learning when the children arrived in school.

The program for home care operations should include such things as the training of home care center operators, the use of observation procedures and TV tape recording of model operations, materials such as books for parents to read to children, the provision of toys on a circulating basis, and aid for trips. The school should consider these home care locations as satellites of the school.

The school also must find time to help mothers, and working mothers in particular, to become effective teachers of their children. The school may well develop, for example, TV taped observations of a child with a description of what the child is doing and what specifically parents can do to assist. The taping of the work of parents with children will provide models or ways in which parents may learn to overcome their own limitations by a discreet review of the recording of their efforts. Joining small groups of parents in a self-help discussion is useful.

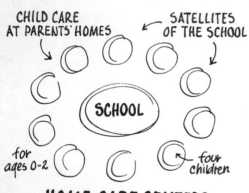

Fig. 1-1 Home care locations should be considered satellites of public schools.

The availability of a skilled child psychologist from the school in working sessions on the upbringing of both very small and older children will be helpful. Again, parents may secure books, toys, or other learning materials. The spaces of the school should be available for fathers and children to work together. Parents should be heavily involved in contributing what they can to the educational program of the school.

THE SCHOOLS AND THE LIBRARY

Where possible, schools should get out of the noninstructional business. The use of public library resources to serve a group of small schools is one way to spread resources more effectively (see Fig. 1-2). Schools will need wide varieties of instructional material, and the care and ordering of such material is a big job. Schools have less use for, and usually poorer resources in, a wide-ranging collection that can be used for varying levels of research. At present most elementary schools are fortunate to have six to ten books in an area of inquiry unless only a few areas are supported by their library resources.

The small schools should be provided with mobile special collections from a central source. These modules of learning materials would include books, magazines, pictures, audio-visual materials, artifacts, samples, and the like of sufficient quantity to saturate a class or group with the learning materials for a topic. The topics, such as Indians or Latin America or the ecology of the community, should be given substantial instead of token support.

The need to do research in depth on a topic is a need met with mockery when the only material available in the school is sharply limited. A substantial collection shared by many schools to which a class might go for a week's intensive study or for some kind of immersion experience might well be vastly superior to the usual 5,000- or 6,000-book school library in which much is promised and little is delivered.

The way in which the roles of the school library and the public library are reviewed and revised is important to education and particularly to elementary schools. There are better uses of the usual resources of professional time and materials than the present arrangement.

THE SCHOOLS AND ADULT EDUCATION

Education is a learning network, and there are strong pressures to continue to learn. The learning exchange and new forms of time- or space-free learning such as college education by television or newspaper are coming

THE SCHOOLS AND THE LIBRARY

Fig. 1-2 The school should get out of the noninstructional business and rely on resources such as the public library for materials and support.

into being, but there are many kinds of learning for which a room or a place to learn is still important.

Every school for young children should have a space for parents. That space can be related to a learning space for adults for use in day or night programs. For example, the school can use the work of many senior citizens. Senior citizens, like any citizens, flourish when needed. If an adult room were available, short periods of work in the school could be interspersed with leisure activities for adults, which would include learning.

CHILD CARE PROGRAM

As shown in Tables 1-1 and 1-2, a simulated program for a child care staff would include operations from 7 to 9 A.M. in the morning, from 11:30 A.M. to 1:00 P.M. in the middle of the day, and from 3:30 to 6:00 P.M., when the center closes. The child care staff opens the school, works with parents as they leave children at school, may furnish breakfast for some children, and provides for pleasant, quiet games and play for most children until school starts. A teacher on the child care staff helps children with homework, as part of the planned program of the total institution to provide extra help to slow-learning children to increase their speed of learning. This help contributes to an improvement in verbal ability, as do the home care center and the continued work with parents.

When the school program opens, the child care staff has a break and then becomes part of the morning program of the school. The aide works with the teacher of the three- to five-year-olds. The recreation teacher becomes the physical education teacher of the morning session. The child care teacher works in the morning mastery learning program.

At noon the morning child care staff is augmented by the afternoon shift. Together they take charge of the midday operation, including lunch and rest for children who need it (rest is certainly necessary for three- to five-year-olds and probably for a number of six- and seven-year-olds). For others after lunch there are quiet games, listening to books being read, and viewing films, followed by vigorous outdoor play. The teachers again may provide help for youngsters in the mastery program. There could be extra work on interests as well.

The child care staff shares in the afternoon school program, as it did in the morning session. The afternoon staff is augmented by part-time aides, who may be parents from the community who bring their children, college students, or, most particularly, high school students who get paid for their services and learn.

TABLE 1-1 STRUCTURE OF A TWELVE-HOUR CHILD CARE—SCHOOL PROGRAM

	Care of young children	School			Total
		Early childhood education	Elementary school		
Age	0 1 2	3 4 5	6 7 8 9 10 11		
Grade equivalent	Home care center	Nursery Kindergarten	1 2 3 4 5 6		
Number	30 30 30	30 30 30	30 30 30 30 30 30		360
Total	90	90	180		360
Number in child care program	40	60	140		240
Child care provision	10 four-child home care centers Operate as satellites of school	Early opening; breakfast for some children Lunch and rest at break at noon at school Afternoon play experience	Early opening; breakfast for some children Lunch, rest, and recreational break Provide help in mastery learning program throughout program as needed Afternoon play experience		
School provision	Help train parents operating satellites	3 groups of 15; 45 children 2 groups of 10; 20 children 1 group with aide, 25 children	Group A; 90 children Group B; 90 children Spend a half day in mastery program alternately with a half day in creative program		

TABLE 1-2 DAY IN A SCHOOL—CARE CENTER

Child care	School	Child care	School	Child care recreation
Early morning activities; breakfast for some children. Help with homework-related mastery program if needed. Children assemble as mothers' work schedules require.		Lunch; rest time for younger children. After lunch reading to children or some recreational break – intramural games, special help, or pursuing interests.		Help some children with school work. Recreation programs, including physical activities, games, arts, music extension; or children are at home if parent is available.
7:00 A.M. 9:00 A.M.		11:30 A.M. 1:00 P.M.		3:30 P.M. 6:00 P.M.
Small number of children; 25 to 180 children	All children	All children	All children	180 children
		School faculty lunch and planning time		

Adult and parent education; work through the day

TABLE 1-3 THE SCHOOL DAY

Time	Early childhood program, age 3 to 5 or 6	Group A, age 5 or 6 to 8 or 9	Group B, age 8 or 9 to 10 or 11
7:00–9:00 A.M.	Child care program	Child care program	Child care program
9:00–11:30 A.M.	90 students organized into 6 groups, with 6 teachers and aide 1 group of 25 children 3 groups of 15 children 2 groups of 10 children	90 students in mastery learning program 1 teacher, reading 1 teacher, mathematics 1 teacher, reading and language skills 1 child care teacher providing special help Diagnostic-prescriptive staff	90 students in creative activities program 1 teacher, social studies 1 teacher, science 1 teacher, art or music 1 teacher, music 1 child care recreation teacher; physical education
11:30 A.M.–1:00 P.M.	Rest	Students in child care program for lunch Rest; quiet play Some help to supplement program	Quiet play; recreation Help in mastery learning program
1:00–3:30 P.M.	Same organization as morning program	90 children in creative study program	90 children in mastery learning program
3:30 P.M.	School closes	School closes	School closes
3:30–7:00 P.M.	Child care program	Child care program	Child care program

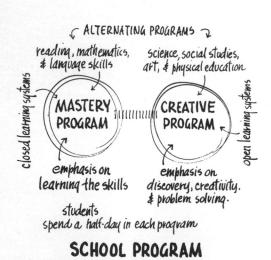

SCHOOL PROGRAM

Fig. 1-3 Both creativity and mastery should be included in planning the curriculum.

SCHOOL PROGRAM

As shown in Tables 1-3 and 1-4, there are no really sharp differences between the school and child care programs. The division is a function of staff deployment and is a convenience in describing the programs. The formal school should be organized in two parts (see Fig. 1-3). One section is a mastery program dealing with reading, mathematics, and language skills; the emphasis is on learning the skills. A very careful track is kept of each student, the key being the amount of time the student spends on a task successfully learning until the material is mastered. The work is carried on in groups of twenty-five, in small groups, and in individualized learning. This is an organized, quiet, serious time with specific goals and with great encouragement for children to succeed.

The other half of the school day may be considered the creative or group part of the program. Social studies, science, art and shop, music, and physical education are involved here, with a program focused on problem solving and the interrelationship of the arts program. Some schools may wish to relate the physical education or movement program to the skills area.

In the model the mastery learning program would involve ninety children, with thirty at each grade or age

TABLE 1-4 STAFFING

Time	Action	Number of children	Child care staff			Formal school staff	
			First group	Activity	Second group	Faculty	Action
7:00 A.M.	School opens	25	1 child care teacher	Organizes; helps children with homework			
			1 aide	Breakfast for children			
			1 recreation teacher	Organizes quiet play			
8:00 A.M.	More children arrive	100	Same staff	Same program			
8:30 A.M.	Children start arriving for formal school	180	Same staff	Program closes; child care staff break		13 teachers	Greet children; talk to parents; compare notes with child care staff
9:00 A.M.	Formal school starts	225	1 recreation teacher	Physical education teacher in morning creativity program		6 teachers	Program for 3–5-year-olds
			1 aide	Becomes aide for 5-year-old program		3 teachers	Mastery program, group A
			1 child care teacher	Works in mastery program		4 teachers	Creativity program, group B
10:30 A.M.	First group, child care staff lunch		Same staff	Lunch			
11:30 A.M.	Formal school stops for lunch and rest; child care program starts noon operation	225	1 recreation teacher	Supervises lunch, play, and games	1 recreation teacher	12 teachers	Lunch hour
			1 aide	Serves and cleans up lunch; supervise rest hours	3 aides		
			1 child care teacher	Helps children in mastery program; reads to children			
1:00 P.M.	Formal school resumes	225		Physical education, P.M.	1 recreation teacher	6 teachers	Afternoon program, 3–5-year-olds
				Aide for young children	1 aide	3 teachers	Mastery program, group B
				Mastery program helps in home care program	2 child care teachers	4 teachers	Creativity program, group A
3:00 P.M.	Child care staff break						
3:30 P.M.	Formal school closes Child care afternoon program starts	180		Games and recreation	1 recreation teacher 2 recreation aides		
				Snacks; care for younger children; supper if needed	5 aides		
				Program for afterschool arts; help for homework	2 child care teachers		
6:00 P.M.	Child care center closes						

level. There would be three teachers skilled in instructional procedures, supplemented by the child care teacher, who has been working informally with the children in other parts of the day.

DIAGNOSTIC-PRESCRIPTIVE SERVICE

A major resource of the mastery program, and one related to the eleven-hour school program, is a diagnostic-prescriptive service. This service processes all formative and summative testing. With the use of test-scoring machines and computer service, all formative tests are subjected to item analysis and marked for correct and incorrect responses. The responses are related to the student's history, and suggestions are printed out for the next study items, including appropriate material for study and the bypassing of learning sequences when this is indicated. If the computer intervention is not available, aides and staff can carry on the same tasks. In any event, a skilled diagnostician and prescription staff member should monitor the process and add in the ingredients of teachers' observations and specialists' diagnoses. The diagnostic and prescriptive service should also provide a summative testing service, keep records of elapsed time in learning, provide data about mastery, and through analysis refine instructional procedures and secure additional help for individual students when this is necessary. A major effort is involved in matching student learning styles and learning materials when computer assistance can be programmed and the resources and experience of the faculty focused on more effective ways of developing a successful match of these two critical factors in the learning process.

THE CREATIVE PROGRAM

The work in social studies and science is an area for group work focused on problem solving. Major emphasis would be placed on the arts, with art and music teachers as regular members of the staff. The model would have ninety students, a teacher of social studies, a teacher of science, a shop and art teacher, a music teacher, and a physical education teacher whose services would be shared with the afternoon child care program.

Alternating Programs

The mastery program and the creative program alternate so that each group spends a half day in each aspect of the school. The mastery program is specific and linear, engages in sequential studies, and uses closed systems where the subject matter is not expected to change rapidly. The creative half of the program deals with open learning systems that, at least in the elementary school, need not be sequential and where the emphasis is on problem solving, putting things together, the creativity of thinking, and the joy of experience.

The yin-and-yang approach can be overdone. The reality is a series of educational experiences that tend to be closer in practice than is suggested in outline, but these are distinctive points of view. The alternation of programs may be changed so that group A has its mastery skills program in the morning one week and in the afternoon another week.

The program in a small school that is suggested here has a linear quality in that the staff concerned with mastery skills deals with a six-year sequence while the creativity sector has an equal time span. No doubt there will be many variations, one being to double the size of the school in order to have twice as many teachers. For example, one team of teachers could deal with beginning skills, and another with more advanced skills. The narrowing of teacher focus may overcome some of the problems involved in the traditional approach, which relies on graded classrooms and the teachers that go with them.

ORGANIZATION OF AN ELEMENTARY SCHOOL– CHILD CARE CENTER

The proposed elementary school is an eleven-hour operation mixing child care and formal elementary education for children from about three years old to about eleven years old (see Fig. 1-4). The formal school program can, of course, be considered separately from the child care operation. The child care program provides for early morning care before school starts. If mothers must start to work very early in the day and families cannot afford breakfast, a simple breakfast may be available in the school. The child care program takes over in a lengthened lunch hour, which includes supervised rest for young children. The regular school faculty has its lunch and planning time at that point. The program in the educational sector resumes in another session in the afternoon that lasts to the usual school-closing hour. The child care staff takes over at that point, operating the school until six o'clock or whatever closing time is appropriate.

The home care centers are operated as satellites of the school. To relate the program in child care time to school

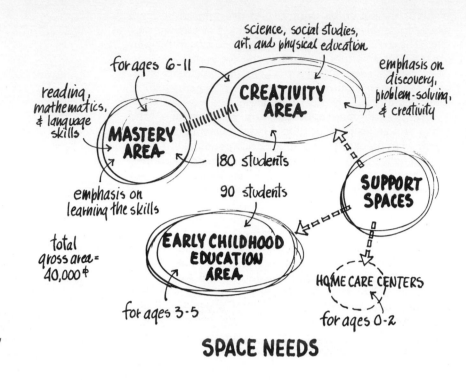

science, social studies, art, and physical education

for ages 6-11

CREATIVITY AREA

emphasis on discovery, problem-solving, & creativity

reading, mathematics, & language skills

MASTERY AREA

180 students

90 students

SUPPORT SPACES

emphasis on learning the skills

total gross area = 40,000 ₵

EARLY CHILDHOOD EDUCATION AREA

HOME CARE CENTERS

for ages 3-5

for ages 0-2

SPACE NEEDS

Fig. 1-4 A total of 40,000 square feet could handle the space needs of an elementary school–child care center.

time, the child care staff may well serve on both staffs. There would necessarily be a two-shift child care staff with an overlap at lunch, and the afternoon staff would be supplemented with part-time people.

SPACE NEEDS

This model school involves eleven hours of time each school day as well as weekend use. It must assiduously cultivate its relationship with parents, both those who use the longer school care program and those who use only the more formal 9:00 A.M.–3:30 P.M. program. The school must find ways to help parents learn how to educate very young children and to help school-age children to learn. It must also interrelate the work of mothers who deal with home child care programs to improve their work, the efforts to aid nonworking mothers to help young children to learn, and the relationships on a very conscious level of the child care provisions for the children of working mothers with the school. The child care program helps children with homework, for example, as good parents help their children. The interrelationship of staffs is significant in accomplishing this aim. Spaces are of particular importance to adults and parents.

This school is dealing with a serious desire to change the ability of each child to learn. In consequence, much of its program is an earnest endeavor to increase concentration on learning, on the more effective use of task time. The reward is a slow but discernible increase in success (or speed) in learning. The mastery area is not a milling confusion. It is a purposeful activity in space that tends to emphasize the quality of the learning going on.

The school has an outgoing, venturesome, put-it-together-and-make-it-work aspect to its creativity program, in which problem solving, group inquiry, simulations, learning games, and the arts are related and integrated into the school day. This space is a mix of studios and laboratories and places where things come together, whether drama or construction or science experiment or social studies activity.

Supporting the school program and found within the school itself are spaces for adult or parent learning, diagnostic and prescriptive services, materials resources, and record keeping.

Outside the school, located in a more centralized fashion, are the food services and research library collections. The data-processing bases that relate materials to the learning styles of the students are centralized. Computer-assisted instruction is centralized in a support center that serves a group of schools; a minicomputer may also be located there. The movement of materials to schools and back to the centralized services is a major concern.

An important problem is that an eleven-hour program and three staff shifts create a desperate need for adequate storage space in the school. Much of the storage should be the wheeled kind that can be moved in and out of large storage spaces so that varieties of programs can be carried on in the same spaces by controlling the use of disposable supplies, projects in process, and the like.

The area for discovery or creativity obviously serves a child care program magnificently as well as a more formal school program. Such a space also serves an adult population. If this is a small local population, the use may be simple and informal. However, the complications of use by another distinctly different group increases the need for storage.

MASTERY LEARNING CENTER

This space (Fig. 1-5) has the equivalent of three classrooms well designed for the presentation of instruction in specific skill areas: reading, mathematics, and language arts. The classrooms relate readily and visually to work space nearby in which students work alone or in small

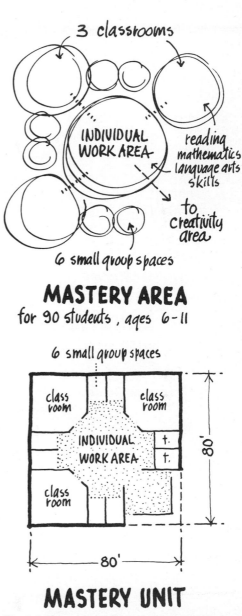

MASTERY AREA
for 90 students, ages 6-11

MASTERY UNIT

Fig. 1-5 The mastery area can be shaped into an 80-square-foot unit with six small group spaces.

groups. Sound control is important. Adjacent to this space is the testing area of the support service.

The open space is used for individualized work. It requires electric power. The space includes work areas for teachers and aides, including a space for a diagnostic-prescriptive specialist. Office landscaping is extensively used, as there are requirements for observation of students at work and for intensive work by students.

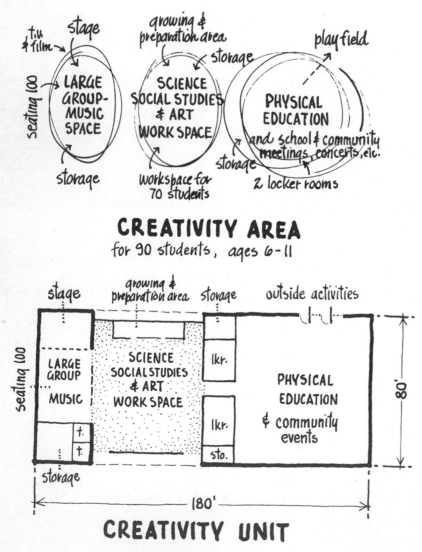

CREATIVITY AREA
for 90 students, ages 6-11

CREATIVITY UNIT

Fig. 1-6 By use of the 80-square-foot space module, the creativity area for ninety students could follow this arrangement.

Mastery Area Spaces

	Square feet
3 classrooms (750 square feet each)	2,250
6 small group spaces (150 square feet each)	900
1 central individualized work area	1,500
Total	4,650

CREATIVITY AREA

This is mostly flexible space designed for active work in science, art and crafts, and social studies, plus space for music and large-group work as well as physical education and movement space (Fig. 1-6). The flexible floor space requires good acoustical conditions but without carpeting in much of the area. Ever-present carpeting has sharply reduced the quality of art, science, and similar programs in schools. The art and science areas need water nearby for student use.

A multipurpose enclosed space for music, large-group meetings, and drama, with a stage that can be used for filming and TV tape recording, is a central unit of this area. The play area, which is used also for movement education, should relate to the early childhood education spaces as well as to the creativity area. Its use for adult education and child care programs makes it a busy place.

Creativity Area Spaces

Large-Group–Music Space

	Square feet	
Seating for 100 (8 square feet each)	800	
Stage or open work space	800	
Storage for music and dance	400	2,000

Science, Social Studies, and Art Work Space

70 students (40 square feet each)	2,800	
Science, growing, and preparation area	400	
Art kiln, project storage, etc.	400	3,600

Physical Education

General area	6,000	
Storage	200	
2 locker rooms (400 square feet each)	800	7,000
Total		12,600

EARLY CHILDHOOD EDUCATION AREA

The program for children three to five years of age is contained in classroom space in conjunction with a common work space (Fig. 1-7). The work space should be full of chances to use water, to grow things, to build great structures, to play, to act, to communicate, and to enjoy. The classrooms should open onto the common work area.

The area for younger children should not be isolated from the older students since students would often cross over.

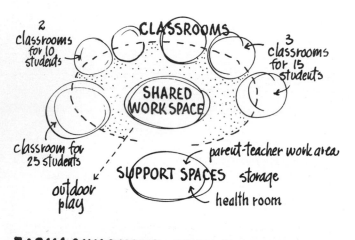

EARLY CHILDHOOD EDUCATION AREA
for 90 students, ages 3-5

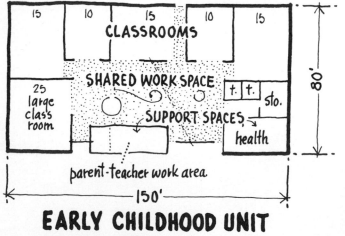

EARLY CHILDHOOD UNIT

Fig. 1-7 The early childhood education area would parallel plans for the creativity and mastery areas. This layout encourages efficiency and unity.

Early Childhood Education Spaces

	Square feet
3 classrooms for 15 students, with toilet, coat storage, storage, and quiet area (1,100 square feet each)	3,300
2 classrooms for 10 students (900 square feet each)	1,800
1 classroom for 25 students (1,400 square feet each)	1,400
General shared work space	2,000

Support Spaces

Parent-teacher work area	300	
Storage	200	
Health room, serving the whole school but near nursery unit	400	900
Total		9,400

SUPPORT SERVICES

The support space (Fig. 1-8) provides room for diagnostic services and the storage of materials for instruction. The wide variety of materials needed to match learning styles with materials is an important function of the support services. The school also should be able to manage food carts delivered to the school as well as library collections provided from centralized sources.

The adult program provides space for parent-teacher conferences, a kind of living room space where groups of people, such as the leaders of home care centers, may discuss problems. A classroom for adult learning programs, adjacent to this space, should be planned for day and evening use, including senior citizen use.

Support Spaces

	Square feet
Test scoring (computer or clerical)	300
Materials storage	1,000
Reception and secretarial	300
Administration	150
2 parent-school conference rooms (100 square feet each)	200

Faculty Space (Child Care, Adult, and Formal School)

Lounge	400	
Lunch area	400	
Work and planning space	400	1,200
Total		3,150

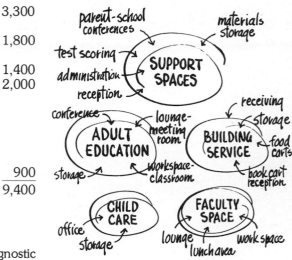

SUPPORT SPACES

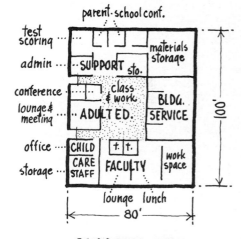

SUPPORT UNIT

Fig. 1-8 Support units would parallel other spaces in the school.

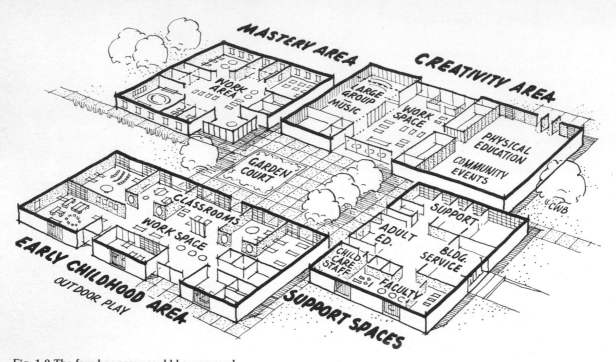

Fig. 1-9 The four key areas could be arranged to form a neighborhood-scale, residential-type cluster on a school-park site. This arrangement would be especially suitable for suburbs and new towns.

Adult Education

	Square feet
Lounge—meeting room	400
2 teacher-parent conference rooms (100 square feet each)	200
Work space—classroom with kitchenette	800
Storage off work space for creativity area	200
Total	1,600

Child Care

	Square feet
Office	200
Storage	400
Total	600

Building Service

	Square feet
Receiving, storage, food cart cleaning, book cart reception and storage, chairs, etc.	1,000

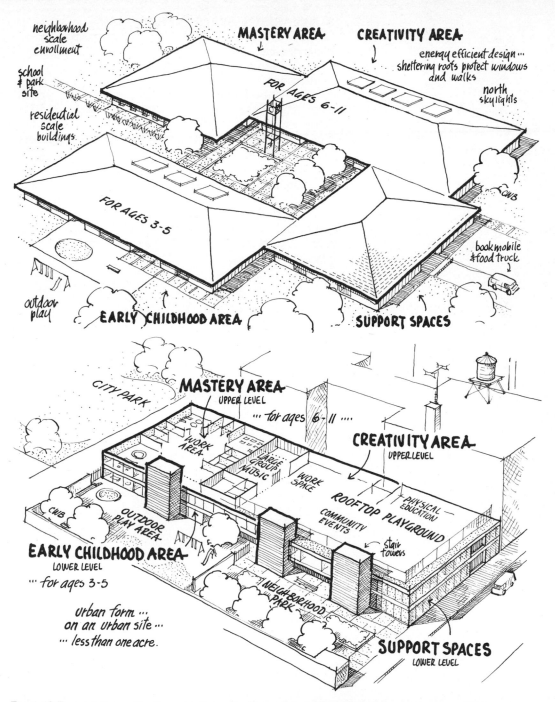

Fig. 1-10 To meet inner-city site restrictions, the four units could be stacked to create a compact two-story structure measuring 80 feet by 260 feet. The lower floor would house the early childhood area and support spaces. The upper floor would contain the mastery and creativity areas.

SUMMARY OF SPACE NEEDS

	Square feet
Mastery area	4,650
Creativity area, including physical education	12,600
Early childhood area	9,400
Support spaces	3,150
Adult education	1,600
Child care	600
Building service	1,000
Net area	33,000
Estimated gross area	40,000

The difference between the net and gross areas is attributable to wall thickness, circulation, building services, and toilets. See Figs. 1-9 and 1-10 for the overall plan of the school.

CHAPTER 2

MODEL MIDDLE SCHOOLS

■ ■ WHAT MAKES A middle school distinctive? The children it serves. Happily, they are neither here nor there. They've escaped from the mother hen atmosphere of the lower grades, but they have not yet been captured by the subject matter orientation of junior or senior high school—not yet been subjugated to scope and sequence. They're literally "between" and temporarily free.

Middle schoolers are insatiable learners, too. They're full of curiosity, energy, and joy. They've progressed to a point in their education at which they're ready to learn about such important things as what makes the world tick. For many, their years at a middle school will be the last time that they can walk all around an issue, looking at it carefully. Once high school subject specialists take over, learning quickly becomes abstract.

In short, middle schoolers are turned-on kids. The task of their school is to capitalize on their energy and freedom by keeping them that way.

To do that, we must recognize that exciting, imaginative ideas and curricula require new models and new ways of thinking about "traditional" learning patterns. No longer can we assume that the best way for children to learn is by moving from the simple to the complex. Motivation, not linear organization, is the prime incentive. It's easier and more exciting to learn to read when children have a good reason of their own to learn than because the school simply says that they should.

If we accept three basic facts about learning, we can develop different patterns of learning experiences: (1) Most of the topics we learn are not sequential; (2) interest motivates and is an enormously valuable support of learning; and (3) thinking is seldom linear but tends to converge around a disturbing area.

Instead of adopting the textbook approach of beginning at the beginning, the middle school curriculum must move toward overviews followed by in-depth study. Then it must proceed to "problem" or "major issue" – oriented structures which reorganize topics so that problems of interest to the student encompass topics that both school and society think are important to learn.

The outcome of following these two approaches will be a student progress matrix showing topics studied in one direction and skills acquired in a second direction. Topics and skills will be brought together by study or problem solving at the intersection of the grids (see Fig. 2-1).

A truly good school will go even further and develop a three-dimensional matrix in which interests at the junction of topics and skills in one plane will be strengthened by a third dimension of talents. This three-dimensional

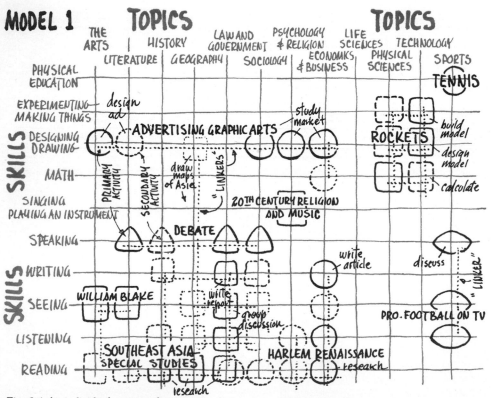

Fig. 2-1 An individual matrix of one student's interests and activities shows how topics and skills are brought together by study or problem solving.

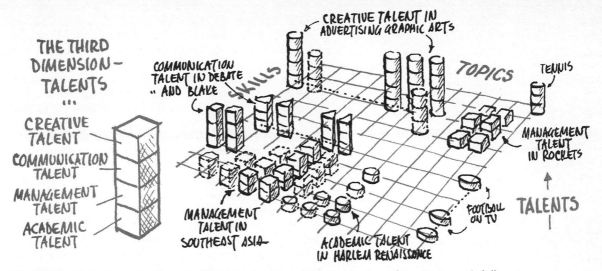

THE THIRD
DIMENSION -
TALENTS

CREATIVE
TALENT

COMMUNICATION
TALENT

MANAGEMENT
TALENT

ACADEMIC
TALENT

CREATIVE TALENT IN
ADVERTISING GRAPHIC ARTS

COMMUNICATION
TALENT IN DEBATE
AND BLAKE

SKILLS

TOPICS

TENNIS

MANAGEMENT
TALENT
IN ROCKETS

TALENTS

MANAGEMENT
TALENT IN
SOUTHEAST ASIA

ACADEMIC TALENT
IN HARLEM RENAISSANCE

FOOTBALL
ON TV

Fig. 2-2 This three-dimensional matrix illustrates how one student's talents reinforce topics and skills.

approach to learning encourages success on a number of
levels. It permits recognition of a variety of talents, such
as creative, communicative, managerial, and academic
abilities (see Fig. 2-2).

There are two basic ways to organize study around
problems. One is to develop the issues within a discipline,
such as by studying, as part of social studies, whether
dissent strengthens or weakens a country. By starting
with a contemporary survey of dissent in differing cultures, it's possible to use history and governmental theory
to illuminate an issue that will continue to be debated.
Another approach is to attack issues which are so broad
that they cut across disciplines and require students to
look at issues from different perspectives.

One such interdisciplinary area of study might be "Can
man survive in the contemporary world?" This would
require students to develop skills and understand concepts from science, social studies, communications, law,
and literature in the course of their investigation.

Another area might be "How can man survive in
space?" This could involve space rocketry design (crafts
and mathematics); space flight (astronomy, meteorol-
ogy); fuel (chemistry, physics); weightlessness (biology,
health care); development (history); costs (economics);
financing (government); and shared projects (international relations).

A third possibility is "How does music reflect current
life-styles?" Study of the guitar, for example, would bring

together many disciplines: the guitar's origin (history); the physics of sound (science); amplification (electronics); record production and sales (manufacturing, advertising, market study, graphic arts, promotion, economics, distribution, and so on); and musical styles (counterpoint, Bach). The study could extend to religious music and religion and, beyond that, to the history of other cultures as reflected through instruments like the sitar.

As these possibilities indicate, middle schools can make learning more exciting by organizing ideas around problems or issues. A common focal point could be the way in which these problems or issues affect people. Teachers would tailor the approach and level of examination to the needs, interests, and capacity of the individual student. The task of the teaching staff would become truly professional: to decide with the student which issues to examine, which approaches to use, and which interrelated ideas and processes to emphasize, and then to set mutually agreed-upon bench marks and goals.

The choice between studying issues set within a discipline and those that are truly interdisciplinary will depend, in part, upon the experience of students and staff. A simple approach would be to begin work within a discipline, broadening the inquiry as students carry it outside the discipline and as the faculty becomes assured that the exercise is resulting in significant learning.

Middle schools, then, can be organized in a variety of exciting ways. Three approaches are suggested here. All are related suborganizations—small in number, responsive to the human scale, and of a size that can be controlled easily by the faculty team.

Model 1

This is an oscillating system in which students in communities move between basic studies and related arts and physical education. Teachers of basic studies have one community of children in the morning and another community in the afternoon. A unified arts team alternates between the communities.

Model 2

This is an immersion system in which students in communities or clusters spend all their time moving between interdisciplinary areas in which basic studies and the arts are intermixed. Each cluster of students has a specialist in communications and a specialist in quantitative studies attached to it. Periodically the cluster moves into different areas of the school in which resident staffs are deeply involved in teaching problem-solving skills.

Model 3

This is a combination of Model 1 and Model 2. A three-year middle school might use Model 1, a self-contained community, for the sixth grade and Model 2, a more highly specialized community, for the seventh and eighth grades.

MODEL 1

THE OSCILLATING SYSTEM

■ ■ IN THIS MODEL (*see* Figs. 2-3 and 2-4), students alternate between basic studies and the related arts and disciplines. An oscillating school of 800 to 1,000 students consists of two subschools of 400 to 500 students, each divided into two communities of 200 to 250 students. Each subschool is made up of one area for basic studies, one area for work in the arts, and an instructional resource center. Using half-day blocks of time, student communities move back and forth between the two major learning areas, stopping periodically at the resource center for independent study and research.

The competencies of teachers and staff in this middle school cluster around two general areas:

1. Basic studies: Social studies, language arts, science, and mathematics. A foreign language can be included. An independent learning coordinator is a member of the basic studies staff.

2. Arts and physical education: art, music, drama and speech, home economics, industrial arts, typing, and physical education.

A teacher's typical day (*see* Table 2-1) looks like this:

8:30–11:00 A.M.	2½-hour teaching block
11:00–11:30 A.M.	team planning
11:30 A.M.–12:30 P.M.	lunch
12:30–2:30 P.M.	2-hour teaching block

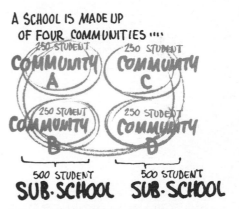

Fig. 2-3 The four basic communities of an oscillating system.

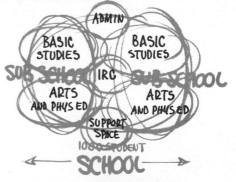

Fig. 2-4 Facilities and the uses to which they are put in an oscillating system.

TABLE 2-1 A TEACHER'S TYPICAL DAY

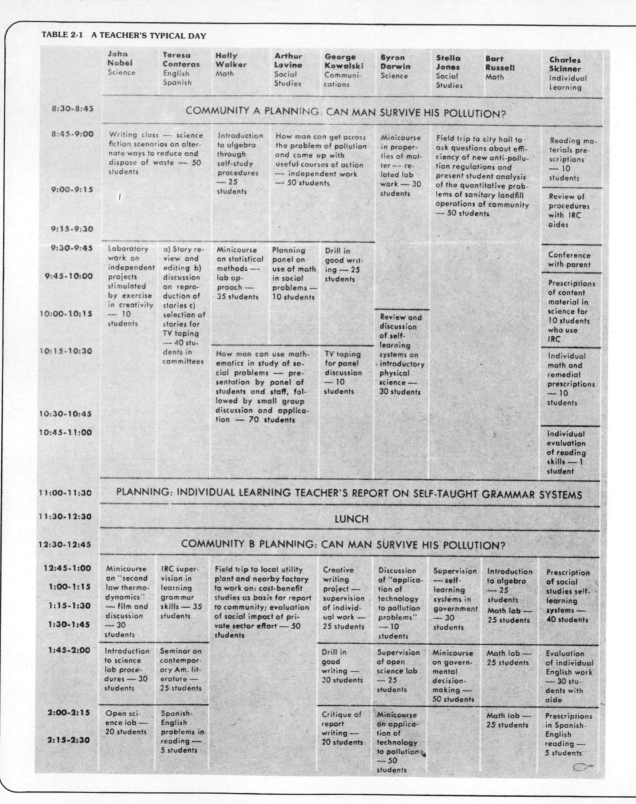

	John Nobel Science	Teresa Conteras English Spanish	Holly Walker Math	Arthur Lavine Social Studies	George Kowalski Communications	Byron Darwin Science	Stella Jones Social Studies	Bart Russell Math	Charles Skinner Individual Learning
8:30–8:45	COMMUNITY A PLANNING: CAN MAN SURVIVE HIS POLLUTION?								
8:45–9:00 9:00–9:15 9:15–9:30	Writing class — science fiction scenarios on alternate ways to reduce and dispose of waste — 50 students		Introduction to algebra through self-study procedures — 25 students	How man can get across the problem of pollution and come up with useful courses of action — independent work — 50 students		Minicourse in properties of matter — related lab work — 30 students	Field trip to city hall to ask questions about efficiency of new anti-pollution regulations and present student analysis of the quantitative problems of sanitary landfill operations of community — 50 students		Reading materials prescriptions — 10 students Review of procedures with IRC aides
9:30–9:45 9:45–10:00 10:00–10:15	Laboratory work on independent projects stimulated by exercise in creativity — 10 students	a) Story review and editing b) discussion on reproduction of stories c) selection of stories for TV taping — 40 students in committees	Minicourse on statistical methods — lab approach — 35 students	Planning panel on use of math in social problems — 10 students	Drill in good writing — 25 students	Review and discussion of self-learning systems on introductory physical science — 30 students			Conference with parent Prescriptions of content material in science for 10 students who use IRC
10:15–10:30 10:30–10:45			How man can use mathematics in study of social problems — presentation by panel of students and staff, followed by small group discussion and application — 70 students		TV taping for panel discussion — 10 students				Individual math and remedial prescriptions — 10 students
10:45–11:00									Individual evaluation of reading skills — 1 student
11:00–11:30	PLANNING: INDIVIDUAL LEARNING TEACHER'S REPORT ON SELF-TAUGHT GRAMMAR SYSTEMS								
11:30–12:30	LUNCH								
12:30–12:45	COMMUNITY B PLANNING: CAN MAN SURVIVE HIS POLLUTION?								
12:45–1:00 1:00–1:15 1:15–1:30 1:30–1:45	Minicourse on "second law thermodynamics" — film and discussion — 30 students	IRC supervision in learning grammar skills — 35 students	Field trip to local utility plant and nearby factory to work on: cost-benefit studies as basis for report to community; evaluation of social impact of private sector effort — 50 students	Creative writing project — supervision of individual work — 25 students	Discussion of "application to pollution technology problems" — 10 students	Supervision — self-learning systems in government — 30 students	Introduction to algebra — 25 students Math lab — 25 students	Prescription of social studies self-learning systems — 40 students	
1:45–2:00	Introduction to science lab procedures — 30 students	Seminar on contemporary Am. literature — 25 students		Drill in good writing — 30 students	Supervision of open science lab — 25 students	Minicourse on governmental decision-making — 50 students	Math lab — 25 students	Evaluation of individual English work — 30 students with aide	
2:00–2:15 2:15–2:30	Open science lab — 20 students	Spanish-English problems in reading — 5 students		Critique of report writing — 20 students	Minicourse on application of technology to pollution — 50 students		Math lab — 25 students	Prescriptions in Spanish-English reading — 5 students	

Within a teaching block, each teacher could teach his own subject at the same time every day. Alternatively, social studies and language arts (and mathematics and science) could be teamed and blocked and even correlated. In a third approach, the entire team could plan its day so that people could vary teaching time according to need.

The way teachers use learning spaces is just as flexible as how they schedule their time.

Instructional Resource Center (IRC)

Here space is provided for individuals and groups to work on independent and small-group projects as well as homework assignments. The idea is to make the space arrangements promote independent study by individuals or small groups. While self-starters and self-directed stu-

TABLE 2-2 A STUDENT WEEK IN MODEL 1

	Monday	Tuesday	Wednesday	Thursday	Friday
8:30-8:45	PLANNING — BASIC STUDIES				
8:45-9:00	Intro to writing science fiction	Intro to algebra minicourse	IRC — skills in reading	Intro to algebra minicourse	Field study
9:00-9:30	Independent work in writing science fiction	Student committee editing science fiction	IRC — learning systems in Am. history	Science discussion seminar	Pollution and government
9:30-10:00	IRC — math skills	IRC — social studies learning system — Am. history	Seminar problem in Am. history	Science lab project	Meeting in town hall with city engineer and city manager
10:00-11:00	Science lab project	Seminar in Am. history	Science lab project	IRC — grammar and spelling — self-testing and skill development	Drafting committee report on field trip
11:00-12:00	PHYSICAL EDUCATION				
12:00-12:30	LUNCH				
12:30-12:45	PLANNING — UNIFIED ARTS				
	Design seminar	Design lab	Design lab	Design lab	Design lab
12:45-1:45	Packaging, industrial design and pollution	Related math and science in developing bio-degradable packaging system			
1:45-2:00	Design lab	Shop: simulations in technology	TV taping of science fiction		Shop: simulations in technology
2:00-2:30	Music chorus				

dents are working on their own in the IRC, others needing individual attention are getting it.

Unlike most secondary school IRCs, which focus almost exclusively on the conceptual, an oscillating middle school IRC should provide skill sequences as well as conceptual ones. Since all students will be in the IRC many times during a given week (see Table 2-2), it would be normal for those needing help and reinforcement to go to the IRC for that purpose as well as for independent study. Individuals need not encounter any opprobrium because of leaving the class group for remedial purposes. The broader IRC concept permits everyone, not merely the very able or the very skilled, to move out of the classroom-like setting.

Basic Studies Area

This space encompasses the disciplines of social studies, language arts, mathematics, and science. Individualized instruction functions in any of these disciplines are handled in the IRC. The basic studies area is the space where students are introduced to problems; where groups discuss how to tackle problems; where analyses are made and results reported; where skills are learned in the context of need; and where the talents of creativity, communication, and management are exercised (see Fig. 2-5).

Art Spaces

Because the arts are arranged around simulations of the world of work, the spaces where simulations are experienced and work information is gained are open spaces, surrounded by skills training areas. This arrangement allows young people to experience to a greater extent how technology, business, the professions, and the arts operate.

Physical Education

Openness, simplicity, and liberal space for a variety of activities are elements in the physical education program.

Fig. 2-5 An open design for a basic studies area (a) accommodates a jumble of activities ranging from staff planning to skill exercises. Also designed with liberal space, the art and physical education area (b) feeds directly into the basic studies area. They combine to create the subschool (c).

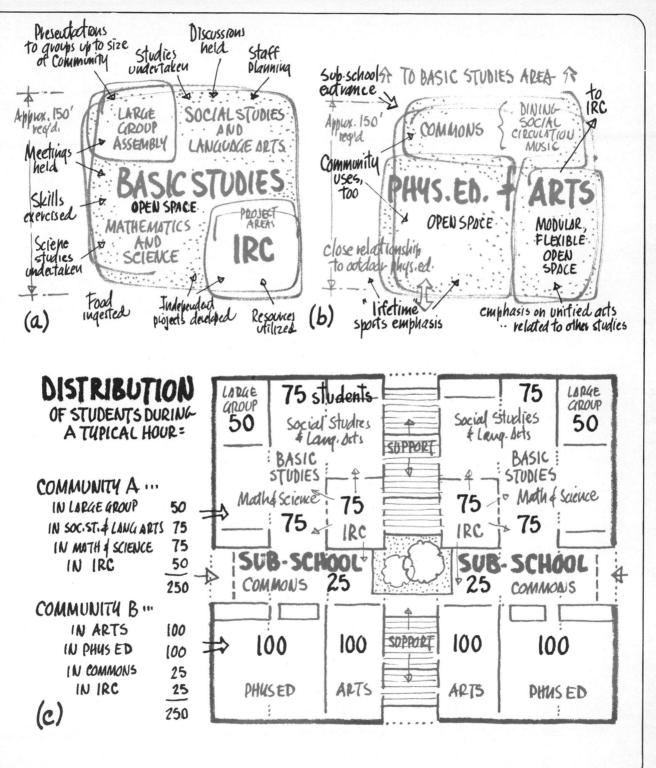

(a)

- Presentations to groups up to size of Community
- Studies undertaken
- Discussions held
- Staff Planning
- Approx. 150' req'd.
- Meetings held
- Skills exercised
- Science studies undertaken
- Food ingested
- Independent projects developed
- Resources utilized

LARGE GROUP ASSEMBLY
SOCIAL STUDIES AND LANGUAGE ARTS
BASIC STUDIES OPEN SPACE
MATHEMATICS AND SCIENCE
PROJECT AREAS IRC

(b)

- Sub-school entrance
- TO BASIC STUDIES AREA
- to IRC
- Approx. 150' req'd
- Community uses, too
- close relationship to outdoor phys.ed.
- "lifetime" sports emphasis
- emphasis on unified arts ·· related to other studies

COMMONS
DINING · SOCIAL · CIRCULATION · MUSIC
PHYS.ED. OPEN SPACE
ARTS MODULAR, FLEXIBLE OPEN SPACE

DISTRIBUTION OF STUDENTS DURING A TYPICAL HOUR:

COMMUNITY A ...

IN LARGE GROUP	50
IN SOC. ST. & LANG ARTS	75
IN MATH & SCIENCE	75
IN IRC	50
	250

COMMUNITY B ...

IN ARTS	100
IN PHYS ED	100
IN COMMONS	25
IN IRC	25
	250

(c)

LARGE GROUP 50
75 students — Social Studies & Lang. Arts
75 — Social Studies & Lang. Arts
LARGE GROUP 50
SUPPORT
BASIC STUDIES — Math & Science
75 — 75
IRC
BASIC STUDIES — Math & Science
75 — 75
IRC
SUB-SCHOOL COMMONS 25
SUB-SCHOOL 25 COMMONS
100
100
SUPPORT
100
100
PHYS ED
ARTS
ARTS
PHYS ED

MODEL 2

THE IMMERSION SYSTEM

■ ■ IN THIS MODEL, students working in clusters utilize interdisciplinary arenas that interrelate the arts and basic studies. Eight clusters of 100 to 125 students circulate through eight arenas that are curriculum centers for in-depth study of problems (see Fig. 2-6). Each cluster is accompanied at all times by two teachers, a communications generalist and a generalist in quantitative studies, both of whom also perform guidance functions (see Table 2-3).

In addition, two teachers are assigned to each interdisciplinary arena. As specialists and artists, they are highly knowledgeable about a series of problems that each arena might deal with. A social studies teacher and a

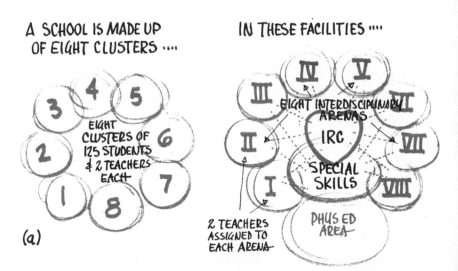

Fig. 2-6 Each cluster *(a)* of students spends approximately four weeks in each problem-oriented interdisciplinary arena *(b)*. An arena's program is developed to mix topics, skills, and disciplines. In the arena for the study of politics of the environment, for example, primary skills are seeing and reading in law and government, economics and business, and life and physical sciences *(c)*.

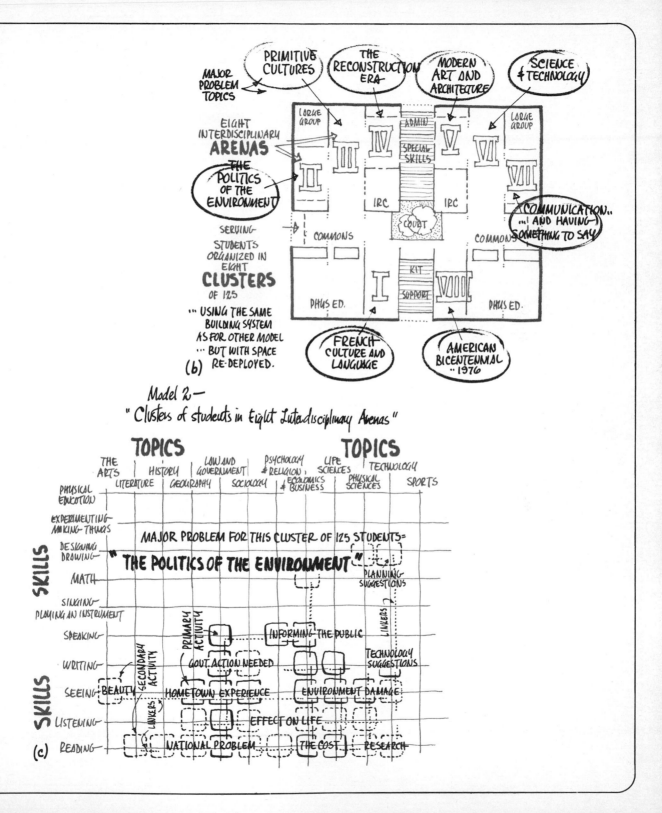

MAJOR PROBLEM TOPICS →

EIGHT INTERDISCIPLINARY **ARENAS**

SERVING STUDENTS ORGANIZED IN EIGHT **CLUSTERS** OF 125

"… USING THE SAME BUILDING SYSTEM AS FOR OTHER MODEL … BUT WITH SPACE

(b) RE-DEPLOYED.

PRIMITIVE CULTURES

THE RECONSTRUCTION ERA

MODERN ART AND ARCHITECTURE

SCIENCE & TECHNOLOGY

THE POLITICS OF THE ENVIRONMENT

"COMMUNICATION… …AND HAVING SOMETHING TO SAY"

FRENCH CULTURE AND LANGUAGE

AMERICAN BICENTENNIAL ·· 1976

Model 2 —
"Clusters of students in Eight Interdisciplinary Arenas"

TOPICS   **TOPICS**

THE ARTS | HISTORY | LAW AND GOVERNMENT | PSYCHOLOGY & RELIGION | LIFE SCIENCES | TECHNOLOGY

LITERATURE | GEOGRAPHY | SOCIOLOGY | ECONOMICS & BUSINESS | PHYSICAL SCIENCES | SPORTS

SKILLS

PHYSICAL EDUCATION
EXPERIMENTING MAKING THINGS
DESIGNING DRAWING
MATH
SINGING PLAYING AN INSTRUMENT
SPEAKING
WRITING
SEEING
LISTENING
READING

MAJOR PROBLEM FOR THIS CLUSTER OF 125 STUDENTS=

"THE POLITICS OF THE ENVIRONMENT"

PLANNING SUGGESTIONS

PRIMARY ACTIVITY

INFORMING THE PUBLIC

LINKERS

GOVT. ACTION NEEDED

TECHNOLOGY SUGGESTIONS

SECONDARY ACTIVITY

BEAUTY | HOMETOWN EXPERIENCE | ENVIRONMENT DAMAGE

LINKERS

EFFECT ON LIFE

NATIONAL PROBLEM | THE COST | RESEARCH

(c)

TABLE 2-3 STAFFING MATHEMATICS OF THE IMMERSION SYSTEM

Staff*	Number
Teachers:	
2 generalists for each of 8 student clusters	16
2 teachers of varied background for each of 8 immersion arenas	16
4 physical education instructors	4
Total	36
Distribution:	
English/communications generalists	8
Mathematics/quantitative studies generalists	8
Arena staff:	
Science	4
Social studies	4
Art	2
Music	2
Home economics/consumer education	2
Technology	2
Physical education	4
Total	36

*In addition, the staff includes the principal, learning resource personnel, aides and part-time specialists, community volunteers, and an independent learning teacher.

technology teacher, for example, might staff arena 5, where youngsters tackle problems of how to keep sources of energy from becoming depleted (see Table 2-4). Each arena is nongraded and has a cycle of study problems that changes about once a year, after eight student clusters have gone through it.

Separate from but easily accessible to the eight arenas are physical education areas, staffed by four people, and instructional resource centers. Without too much difficulty, satellite IRCs could be attached to each arena. This would enable both students and teachers to investigate various aspects of their current problem-oriented topic with great ease.

Staffing

Utilizing a systems approach, the staff is made up of an interesting mixture of specialists and generalists. Subject matter teachers (specialists) stay in the arenas where their skills are best used. Roving faculty members (experienced generalists) stay with students, traveling from arena to arena and learning as much as their students do.

TABLE 2-4   BROAD TOPICS FOR A THREE-YEAR CYCLE OF STUDY

	FIRST YEAR	SECOND YEAR	THIRD YEAR
ARENA 1 Social studies Science	Can man survive in his polluted environment?	Organic farming and U.S. farm policy	Transportation in the future
ARENA 2 Art Technology	A simulation of technology	How to design and build street furniture for tomorrow's world	Will design and technology improve the quality of human living?
ARENA 3 Social studies Music	The guitar and its social and cultural setting	What will it take to produce a new Renaissance?	Rock music and cultural unrest: cause or result?
ARENA 4 Science Home economics	The scientist and family life education	Consumer education: a laboratory approach	What science and education can do to help in early development of children
ARENA 5 Social studies Technology	Will our sources of energy be depleted?	The social need for new housing technology	Communications technology and social policy
ARENA 6 Science Art	Art and nature: a sense of wonder	Design and the technological future	The computer and art
ARENA 7 Social studies Home economics	How can we develop more effective delivery systems for nutrition?	How can we develop more effective delivery systems for health?	How can we develop more effective political decision-making?
ARENA 8 Science Music	The scientific basis of the study of noise or acoustics	How to develop new musical instruments	Music as mathematics

Topics studied in the arenas relate directly to the subject specialties of teachers who staff the arenas. Indirectly, each topic also relates to English/communications and quantitative studies. The need to read, for example, becomes all the more urgent as students find themselves in open-ended inquiry settings. And work within the arenas requires that students know how to write reports, discuss and understand the literature.

The skill teachers in communications and mathematics, who move from arena to arena with students, have the responsibility to develop sequential portions of the skill-learning tasks. Their work is made more effective by the frequency with which they can help students put their skills to work in the arenas.

MODEL 3

THE OSCILLATING AND IMMERSING SYSTEM

■ ■ WITHIN A SINGLE 1,000-student school, it's possible to operate a coordinated program that combines Model 1 and Model 2 without creating competing systems. In this arrangement, Model 1 subschools, consisting of two 250-student communities, are linked to the Model 2 area by the two instructional resource centers. Clusters of 125 students work in each of the four Model 2 areas (see Fig. 2-7).

One advantage of the combined system is that it provides opportunities for both staff and students to find the model that works best for them. Another is that the staff can recharge its batteries and broaden its teaching and learning experiences by spending a semester in each model on an exchange basis. As the staff grows familiar with both models, decisions about who goes where for how long can be based on its experience and the results of student testing.

Fig. 2-7 Two models exist side by side, linked by twin instructional resource centers.

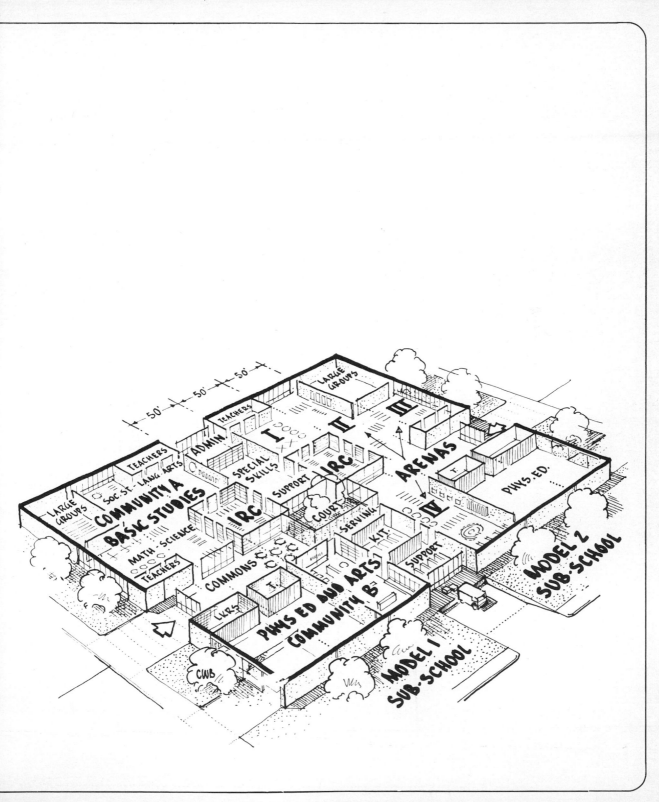

CHAPTER 3

THE CASE FOR A SMALL HIGH SCHOOL

■ ■ WHAT HAPPENS IF you plan a high school for a maximum of 250 students? Ask most educators, and they'll frown, especially if they were weaned on the Conant dictum that high schools of fewer than 750 students don't count.

A lot of first-rate schools across the country are big, but a lot of big schools across the country are not first-rate. "There is something about largeness that attracts more problems," said a principal who was quoted in *Education USA,* "but we continue to build larger and larger schools."

It makes sense to consider a small secondary school for a variety of reasons, including these:

- Because a small school is small, each student is really needed. This need creates an important counterbalance to our impersonal culture.
- New curriculum developments, which take into account reorganized programs and human talent, can help make a small school workable and desirable.

Here is a look at a projected program that could be adopted by small secondary schools of 250 or fewer students (down to a minimum of 50). Called the Smallway model, it is based on the premise that small schools can compete successfully with larger ones and provide an effective range of experiences for students if (1) the teaching model is shifted and (2) four organizational devices now being used can be synchronized.

Although the program is designed for a small school,

the approaches it embodies can be applied to larger schools contemplating "house" plans or other types of internal organization that seek to foster smallness and a more personal education.

THE TEACHING MODEL

With ten faculty members plus a combination principal-counselor and a librarian-teacher, the small high school could readily handle 200 to 250 students. The pupil-professional staff ratio of from 17 to 20 to 1 is competitive with usual practice, opening up opportunities for individual and small-group instruction. What's more, the small high school can offer seventy or more courses yearly with greater flexibility than larger schools.

At Smallway the teacher must shift his approach and become a guide to learning, forgoing the satisfaction of transmitting knowledge. With this model, a class of at least twenty students is not needed to offer a given course efficiently. Moreover, a huge base of students is unnecessary to provide the interested or gifted few with the most highly specialized course in a sequence. By developing approaches with which students may learn at their own speed, advanced-placement physics or calculus, for example, can be offered to one, two, or ten students.

The same theory and student-staff ratio can be applied to larger secondary schools simply by doubling, tripling, or quadrupling the program.

When hiring teachers for Smallway, start with the variety of talents wanted rather than a particular quota. This variety will determine the size of the staff, which in turn will determine the approximate student population.

Ten to twelve staff members provide the framework on which to build a program. The following talents are to be presented (see also Fig. 3-1):

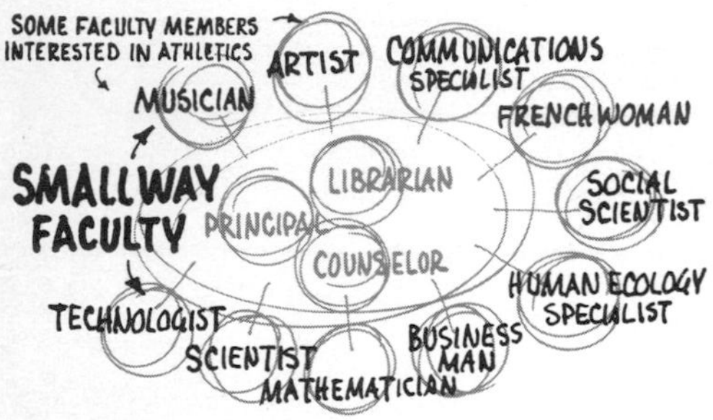

- Artist
- Businessman
- Communications and literary expert
- Home economics specialist
- Language instructor
- Mathematician
- Musician
- Scientist
- Social scientist
- Technologist
- One or two teachers interested in athletics

Employing one good general scientist instead of a number of specialized scientists is a key suggestion. It may be comforting to have a biophysicist, biologist,

Fig. 3-1 The staff of Smallway is made up of faculty generalists flanking the principal, counselor, and librarian. The principal also assumes a counseling function, and the librarian is a part-time teacher.

chemist, or physicist on the staff, but qualified specialists are not always available or used effectively when they are found. It may be better to have one scientist, whatever his specialty, who understands scientific procedures and processes and can transfer these concepts to students, with suggestions on how to plan a scientific endeavor.

Because Smallway lacks some subject specialists, it should not rely solely on in-house staff. The community has an infinite number of professionals who can widen students' areas of knowledge and provide them with apprenticeships in specific fields. What scientist or doctor or engineer or musician would turn down a sincere invitation to "come out and help the kids"?

ORGANIZATIONAL PATTERNS

There are four related organizational devices[1] that make Smallway economically and practically feasible, allowing it to compete successfully with larger schools while providing an effective range of experiences for students. These are:

1. Phasing, a proposal that all the students of the school study one major curriculum topic at a time. Phasing assumes a nongraded structure, questioning the validity of having a ninth-grade course that differs from one for tenth-grade students.

For example, in the area of social studies, the school might offer three major courses. American history, world studies, and government. The school would schedule these in different years, and all students would take them at the same time. This procedure eliminates the need to offer all three courses each year, thus allowing the faculty to teach a wider variety of subjects over the three- or four-year high school cycle. In addition, it enhances the sense of community for the students, who operate more nearly as a total body.

Although phasing is proposed, state requirements may dictate that certain courses be repeated at least every other year for the benefit of incoming students.

2. Short-term minicourses reject the theory that in order to take a subject you must spend a year or more at it. The inoculation period, in fact, is a good deal shorter, perhaps nine, six, or even as few as three weeks. A minicourse on the Great Depression, for example, taken as an adjunct to American history, directs students' interests to a specific area of knowledge under an overall

---

[1]Taken from "A Proposal for an Innovative Secondary Education Program for Bratenahl, Ohio," Stanton Leggett and Associates, Inc., Chicago, November 1969.

heading. A short course might also involve a skill, such as weaving, under home economics.

3. A nongraded approach must also be a basic part of Smallway. Whenever we do anything that counts in education, we ungrade, mixing the experienced with the inexperienced. This allows us to gain stability and continuity and to make sure that students teach other students.

All performance areas—band, football, cheerleading, dramatics—are organized in this fashion because success is vital. Jobs are at stake. But what may be even more important, an ungraded school allows students of varying abilities to proceed at their own pace.

4. Uncommitted time in the learning schedule is the fourth guidepost. The student who races from class to class is not being provided with time to think, and the typical crowded six-period day eliminates thinking, time to study, time to visit the library, and time to do anything except listen to teachers.

A considerable amount of time is left open for both students and teachers to use at their discretion. A portion of this time may be utilized for independent study; some can be used for unscheduled student-teacher meetings; and open laboratory time may be arranged so that students can work on their projects in any available facility.

Smallway's Rationale: How Large Is Good? How Good Is Small?

It is widely accepted that the small high school has severe limitations in diversity of curricular and extracurricular programs. Consequently, American educators, unable to solve the constrictions of the small school, have urged school consolidation with considerable success.

The prevailing idea of the appropriate size of high schools has risen sharply over the years. Intuition, authority, and the American passion for size provide us with a numbers game: high schools should have no less than 750, or 1,250, or 1,500, or 1,800, or 2,200 students. This drift toward largeness has been based upon a rigid interpretation of class size, grade level, and the role of the teacher as dispenser of information. The basic educational package has been twenty-five students, at a particular grade, in a narrow subject area, taught one period every day for a year. With these criteria, to be able to offer specialized classes—fifth-year French, advanced-placement physics—actually does require a very large base number of students.

However, there can be a different base on which to determine effective and efficient size. This base is provided by modern educational procedures, in which the student takes on the responsibility for learning, the teacher becomes a guide in the learning process, and much information is transferred through well-designed books, audio-visual materials, programmed texts, and similar learning devices. With individualized instruction, nongraded and phased approaches to instruction, and independent study, a properly organized small high school can offer a much more diverse education, more closely related to the needs of the individual, than can the traditional large high school, and probably at no greater cost.

It is the view of the Smallway proposal that with creative use of present technological and conceptual breakthroughs, many of the severely damaging limitations of large and small school size can be eliminated. The students and staff can benefit from the obvious and subtle advantages of smallness in a culture drowning in a sea of impersonality.

As our institutions have grown larger in accordance with the intuitive, auditor-type notion that the larger the institution the cheaper and the better, our problems in society have increased. Student unrest has been, at least in part, a rejection of the gigantic. One wonders whether the presumed savings on teaching staff in the large high schools have been offset by the necessity to hire security staff and whether the supposed effectiveness of size, in terms of more numerous offerings to the students, is offset in their minds by the clutter of rules and regulations needed to keep a large school going.

Smallway offers one more option: school districts can consider or modify themselves in terms of their needs and available community resources.

HOW FACULTY AND STUDENTS ARE SCHEDULED

Two general statements may be made about Smallway's schedule: (1) Teachers will find that the number of preparations has decreased, permitting them to carry a more reasonable work load and to enjoy more time for individualized instruction; and (2) students cannot help but be exposed to a greater variety of classroom experiences coupled with the flexibility of independent study.

Faculty Load

Most schools ask teachers to teach five or six out of six hours a day. In an average week, a teacher talks at students for about twenty-five to thirty hours.

A typical Smallway teacher, however, has only three

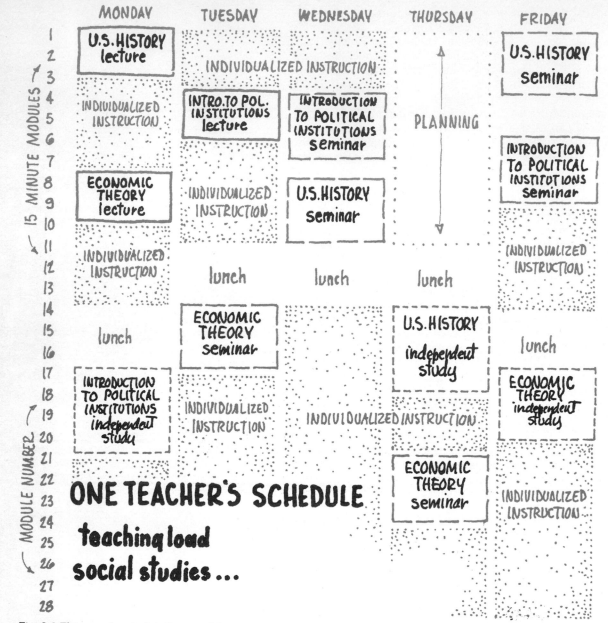

	MONDAY	TUESDAY	WEDNESDAY	THURSDAY	FRIDAY
1	U.S. HISTORY lecture	INDIVIDUALIZED INSTRUCTION		PLANNING	U.S. HISTORY seminar
2					
3					
4	INDIVIDUALIZED INSTRUCTION	INTRO. TO POL. INSTITUTIONS lecture	INTRODUCTION TO POLITICAL INSTITUTIONS seminar		
5					
6					INTRODUCTION TO POLITICAL INSTITUTIONS seminar
7					
8	ECONOMIC THEORY lecture	INDIVIDUALIZED INSTRUCTION	U.S. HISTORY seminar		
9					
10					
11	INDIVIDUALIZED INSTRUCTION				INDIVIDUALIZED INSTRUCTION
12		lunch	lunch	lunch	
13					
14					
15	lunch	ECONOMIC THEORY seminar		U.S. HISTORY independent study	lunch
16					
17	INTRODUCTION TO POLITICAL INSTITUTIONS independent study				ECONOMIC THEORY independent study
18					
19		INDIVIDUALIZED INSTRUCTION	INDIVIDUALIZED INSTRUCTION		
20					
21					
22				ECONOMIC THEORY seminar	INDIVIDUALIZED INSTRUCTION
23					
24					
25					
26					
27					
28					

15 MINUTE MODULES

MODULE NUMBER

ONE TEACHER'S SCHEDULE

teaching load
social studies ...

Fig. 3-2 This sample schedule for a social studies teacher shows large blocks of time for individualized instruction, a minimum of course preparation, and a half day (Thursday morning) devoted to planning.

courses meeting three hours per week. On a noncourse basis he or she helps five to ten students in dealing with issues that are within his or her area of competence. This help would be given through individualized work plus group seminars.

Here is one proposal for organizing the teacher load (see also Fig. 3-2).

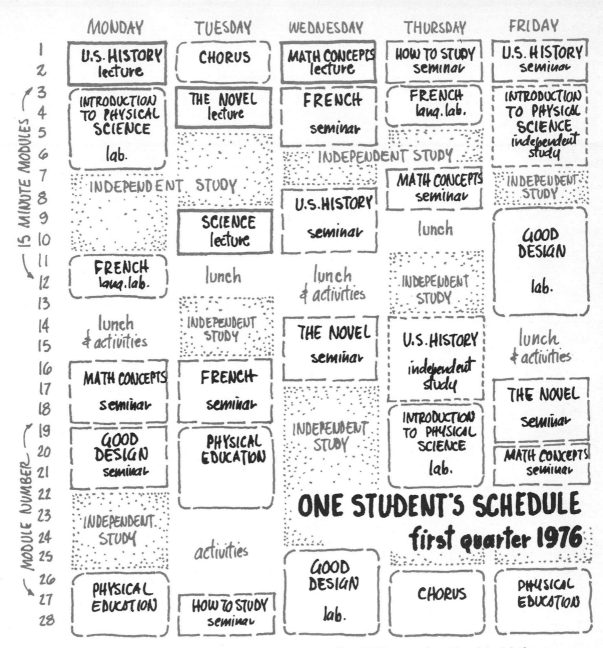

	MONDAY	TUESDAY	WEDNESDAY	THURSDAY	FRIDAY
1 2	U.S. HISTORY lecture	CHORUS	MATH CONCEPTS lecture	HOW TO STUDY seminar	U.S. HISTORY seminar
3 4 5 6	INTRODUCTION TO PHYSICAL SCIENCE lab.	THE NOVEL lecture	FRENCH seminar	FRENCH lang. lab.	INTRODUCTION TO PHYSICAL SCIENCE independent study
7 8	INDEPENDENT STUDY		INDEPENDENT STUDY	MATH CONCEPTS seminar	INDEPENDENT STUDY
9 10		SCIENCE lecture	U.S. HISTORY seminar	lunch	GOOD DESIGN lab.
11 12 13	FRENCH lang. lab.	lunch	lunch & activities	INDEPENDENT STUDY	
14 15	lunch & activities	INDEPENDENT STUDY	THE NOVEL seminar	U.S. HISTORY independent study	lunch & activities
16 17 18	MATH CONCEPTS seminar	FRENCH seminar	INDEPENDENT STUDY		THE NOVEL seminar
19 20 21	GOOD DESIGN seminar	PHYSICAL EDUCATION	INDEPENDENT STUDY	INTRODUCTION TO PHYSICAL SCIENCE lab.	MATH CONCEPTS seminar
22 23 24 25	INDEPENDENT STUDY	activities			
26 27 28	PHYSICAL EDUCATION	HOW TO STUDY seminar	GOOD DESIGN lab.	CHORUS	PHYSICAL EDUCATION

15 MINUTE MODULES

MODULE NUMBER

ONE STUDENT'S SCHEDULE
first quarter 1976

Fig. 3-3 This sample student schedule for one quarter illustrates the possible variety of courses made available by the shorter (fifteen-minute) modules, with much time left over for independent study.

- Each module is fifteen minutes.
- Each course, or organized offering, takes three hours of teacher contact time weekly, supplemented by reading, research, and individualized work.
- Each teacher has three of these course offerings.
- Each teacher is responsible for individualized work

with five to ten students, perhaps involving four to six course areas.

Student Load

The student program for Smallway is substantial, varying with the individual's capability and level of operation (see Fig. 3-3). Since the school day offers the students time to think about what they are doing and time to seek help if needed, they can involve themselves in more of the intellectual fare of the school while also developing a broad range of nonintellectual talents. For example, the small school is organized so that late-afternoon modules are devoted to sports, recreation, and music, again mixing faculty and students on a quality basis.

The expectations are that most students would take eight or nine subjects each quarter, including physical education, music, art, and independent study. Substantially greater amounts of course work are scheduled for independent study, as shown on the sample student schedule in Fig. 3-3. A portion of this time set aside for independent study may be used for meetings with teachers or for open laboratories arranged so that students may work on projects in their uncommitted time in any available facility. Subjects that lend themselves to the open laboratory concept are art, science, shorthand or typing, music, and language.

WHAT KIND OF PROGRAM?

What kind of instructional program can be managed by as few as ten teachers and 200 students? The Smallway answer is a very flexible and varied one, as shown by the schedules of suggested course offerings for three consecutive years, broken down into four quarters per year, in Table 3-1.

The program, based on a schedule of fifteen-minute modules, is designed to exceed or meet most state standards for high schools. Even with a staff of no more than ten full-time teachers, Smallway can provide more than seventy units of study each year and more than 200 different courses in three years, without considering independent or tutorial options.

The only part of the master schedule that remains constant from year to year is the domains, or general bodies, of knowledge. It is noteworthy that the number of domains (eleven) approximates the number of Smallway faculty members.

The phased approach provides at least thirty-seven different courses in any given quarter. In addition, all

TABLE 3-1 SUGGESTED SMALLWAY SCHOOL COURSE OFFERINGS

Domains of knowledge	1976–1977 quarters			
	1	2	3	4
Social studies	United States history: overview*	The Civil War[B]	Reconstruction[E]	The Roaring Twenties[H]
	Introduction to political institutions[A]	Stones and bones (archaeology)	Introduction to sociology and anthropology*	Black history[J]
	Economic theory	Consumer economics*	Liberty in the American culture[F]	American government and political institutions*
Humanities and language arts	Introduction to philosophy	Camus; Sartre[C]	*On Liberty; Darkness at Noon; Travels with Charley*[F]	Poetry[J]
	The novel*	*The Red Badge of Courage;*[B] *Gone with the Wind; Andersonville*	*The Adventures of Huckleberry Finn; Silent Grow the Guns*[E]	*The Great Gatsby;*[H] *Babbitt; Babylon Revisited*
	Paragraph development	Introduction to speech*	Grammatical systems*	Introductory composition
	How to study*	Vocabulary building	Phonetics	Fundamentals of spelling
Science	Introduction to physical science* ⟶			
	Physics ⟶			
	Laboratory technics	Microbiology	The fetal pig	Photography
Foreign language	French I ⟶			
	French II ⟶			
	French literature; Voltaire[A]	Camus; Sartre[C]	Montaigne[E]	Contemporary French poetry[J]
	Comparative languages; Russian	Japanese	Chinese	Swahili
Mathematics	Fundamental concepts of mathematics* ⟶			
	Algebraic concepts ⟶			
	Introduction to statistics	The slide rule	Probability[G]	Topics
Business	Personal and business typing ⟶			
	Data processing	Unit equipment	Programming[G]	Business law
	The American business firm[D]	Systems analysis[D]	Notehand	
	Work experience ⟶			

(continued)

TABLE 3-1 SUGGESTED SMALLWAY SCHOOL COURSE OFFERINGS (Continued)

Domains of knowledge	1976–1977 quarters			
	1	2	3	4
Industrial arts	The industrial enterprise simulation[T] ——————→ Electronics			
	Woods and metals ——————→ Power mechanics			
	Technical drawing ————————————————————————————→			
	Work experience ————————————————————————————→			
Home economics	Foods and nutrition I ——————→ Foods and nutrition II ———————→			
	Clothing I ——————→ Clothing II ————————————————→			
	Nutrition	Child development	Chef's course (men only)	Interior design
Art	Good design ——————→ Workshop (in basic skills) ————————→			
	Composition	Sculpture	Metals	Black art[l]
	Sketching	Watercolors	Oils	Metal sculpture
Music	String quartet I ————————————————————————————→			
	Chorus I ————————————————————————————→			
	Harmony	The romantic period	Folk music	Composition
Physical education	Physical education ————————————————————————→			
	Modern dance† ————————————————————————→			
	Golf†	Bowling	Tennis	Table tennis; badminton
	Health* ————————————————————————————→			
	1977–1978 quarters			
Social studies	The Great Depression[K]	The atomic age: alienation and society[M]	History of political thought and dissent[P]	The Revolution of 1776[P]
	Sub-Saharan Africa[L]	Minority people[M]	Criminology	Urban problems[S]
	The American and Ohio constitutions*	Introduction to adolescent psychology[N]	The Romans[R]	The Renaissance[T]
Humanities and language arts	The Grapes of Wrath; Tobacco Road[K]	The Pearl; Black like Me; Native Son; Dangling Man; Catcher in the Rye; Black Rage[M]	Oliver Twist; Les Miserables; 12 Angry Men[Q]	The Divine Comedy[T]
	The theater	Hamlet; A Separate Peace[N]	Meditations; Julius Caesar[R]	Death of a Salesman; Raisin in the Sun; Two Blocks Apart; Manchild in the Promised Land[S]
	History of the English language*	Writing the short story	Thoreau[P]	Humorous verse
	Roots and stems: building vocabulary	Effective sentences*	Semantics	Specific forms of composition

TABLE 3-1   SUGGESTED SMALLWAY SCHOOL COURSE OFFERINGS (Continued)

Domains of knowledge	1977–1978 quarters			
	1	2	3	4
Science	Biology ⟶			
	Chemistry ⟶			
	Optics	Paleontology	Advanced topics	Histology
Foreign language	French I ⟶			
	French II ⟶			
	French III ⟶			
	French literature; history of France	Descartes; *Les Miserables*[Q]		*Penguin Island*
Mathematics	Advanced algebraic concepts ⟶			
	Geometry ⟶			
	Mathematical games	Geometrical systems	Systems of logic	Special topics
Business	Personal and business typing II ⟶			
	Shorthand ⟶			
	Administrative procedures	Organization of business	Bookkeeping techniques ⟶	
	Work experience I and II ⟶			
Industrial arts	Industrial simulation ⟶		Power mechanics II ⟶	
	Electricity ⟶		Plastics	Jewelry
	Technical drawing II ⟶			
	Work experience I and II ⟶			
Home economics	Child development practicum ⟶		Family finance	Meats
	Family relationships ⟶		Foreign foods	Gourmet cooking
	Kitchen and dining area planning	Baked products	Shelter design	Consumer problems
Art	African art[L]	Modern art[M]	Ancient art and art forms[R]	Renaissance art[T]
	Enameling	Plastics	Workshop in advanced skills ⟶	
	Early-twentieth-century American art	Lapidary arts	Sculpture II	Crafts
Music	String quartet I and II ⟶			
	Chorus I and II ⟶			
	Opera	Musical comedy	Children's music	Theory

(continued)

TABLE 3-1 SUGGESTED SMALLWAY SCHOOL COURSE OFFERINGS (Continued)

Domains of knowledge	1977–1978 quarters			
	1	2	3	4
Physical education	Physical education† ⟶			
	Modern dance† ⟶			
	Field hockey and handball	Folk dance performance group	Basketball and soccer skills	Gymnastics and tumbling
	1978–79 quarters			
Social studies	United States history: overview*	The old West[W]	Military history	Russia before the Czars[AA]
	World population pressures	Consumer economics*	Introduction to sociology and anthropology*	The Greeks[BB]
	Japan through the ages[U]	Preliterate people	How to Make a Million	American government and political institutions*
Humanities and language arts	The novel*	*The Virginian, Leatherstocking Tales; The Luck of Roaring Camp;[W] The Robber Barons; The Jungle; The Oxbow Incident*	Poetry*[X]	Russia: *Dr. Zhivago; War and Peace; The Brothers Karamazov*[AA]
	Far Eastern literature[U]		Elizabethan drama[Y]	*The Flies; Meno; The Republic;* Herodotus; Thucydides; *The Iliad*[BB]
	Haiku[U]	Introduction to speech*	Debate and persuasion	The drama*
	Mechanics of research	Interpretive writing	Verse writing	Drama workshop
Science	Introduction to physical science* ⟶			
	Advanced physics ⟶			
	Projects: biology	Anatomy	Zoology	Botany
Foreign language	French I ⟶			
	French II ⟶			
	French III ⟶			
	French literature; *Germinal*	Anouilh	French poetry[X]	Racine
Mathematics	Fundamental concepts of mathematics* ⟶			
	Calculus ⟶			
	Algrebraic concepts ⟶			
	Tools of mathematics	Trigonometry	Logic and Venn diagrams	Data processing;[CC] programming
Business	Personal and business typing ⟶			
	Shorthand and notehand ⟶			
	Organization and administration of the corporation ⟶		Business law	Data processing[CC]

TABLE 3-1   SUGGESTED SMALLWAY SCHOOL COURSE OFFERINGS (Continued)

Domains of knowledge	1978–1979 quarters			
	1	2	3	4
Business (cont'd)	Work experience I, II, and III ⟶			
Industrial arts	The industrial enterprise simulation ⟶ Woods ⟶			
	Graphics			
	Technical drawing ⟶ Crafts			Leather making
	Work experience I, II, and III ⟶			
Home economics	Foods I ⟶ Foods II ⟶			
	Clothing I ⟶ Clothing II ⟶			
	Landscaping	Salads and desserts	Textile design^Z	Weaving
Art	Good design ⟶ Workshop ⟶			
	Far Eastern art^U	Sketching	Oils ⟶	
	Composition	Landscapes and seascapes	Art and textiles^Z	Classical art^{BB}
Music	String quartet ⟶			
	Chorus ⟶			
	Triple trio	Bach; Beethoven; Brahms	Shakespearean and English music	Guitar
Physical education	Physical education† ⟶			
	Modern dance† ⟶			
	Teaching games†	Bowling	Ballet	Golf
	Health* ⟶			

*Required.
†One required.
Note: Letters A–CC indicate correlated or interdisciplinary programs. In the humanities the books cited are merely suggested examples.

students are required to pursue one unit of credit each year in independent work. Even with phasing, some required courses must be repeated at least every other year to meet state requirements for incoming students. United States history, for example, is offered in the first quarter of 1976–1977 and in the first quarter of 1978–1979.

Provision for interdisciplinary experiences is perhaps the key feature of the schedules. If a particular unit has a footnoted letter, look for one or more units footnoted with the same letter under other domains of knowledge in the same year. A guide such as this enables the student to select courses that will provide him with many more insights into a specific subject. For example, the Renaissance is offered under social studies in the fourth quarter of 1977–1978. It is footnoted with a *T*. A second *T* appears in the same quarter under the domain of art, and the course is, as you would suspect, Renaissance art. The two courses may be taught separately or be combined into one course that is team-taught by the social studies, language, art, and music teachers to provide a unique interdisciplinary inquiry into this era's people and culture.

In addition, several block-type interdisciplinary courses might be included as alternates or additions. One, for example, could be called "Now!" This would be an extensive analysis of the environment, focusing on communications by various media, urban problems, pollution, and other interdisciplinary elements. Two or three modules a week could be used for this program.

Year-long courses (taken for all four quarters of a year) are also provided in certain domains in which a longer learning period is needed, such as business, science, music, and physical education. In many cases even the semester study approach can be richly varied, for the student may take an overview of United States history the first quarter and then select from a number of specialized minicourses—the old West, the Roaring Twenties, the Great Depression—for the second, third, and fourth quarters.

The nature of the proposed program, as illustrated by three consecutive years of master schedules, is clear. What is not shown is the wide range of possible individualized programs. The slow learner has time, with the help of staff and materials, to work toward greater achievement. And for the very able student, the entire three years is a stimulating honors program.

HOW MUCH DOES SMALLWAY COST?

In terms of costs, Smallway has been designed to be comparative with the normal-size high school. With ten faculty members plus a combination principal-counselor and a librarian-teacher, the faculty could readily handle 200 to 250 students. The pupil-professional staff ratio is around or a little better than the national average, and the staff salary costs per student would therefore remain competitive.

Software and audio-visual equipment may be more costly on a per pupil basis. This cost can be reduced, by shared supply and equipment plans, if other schools are located close by. Moreover, if the system is properly promoted within the community, post-high school pro-

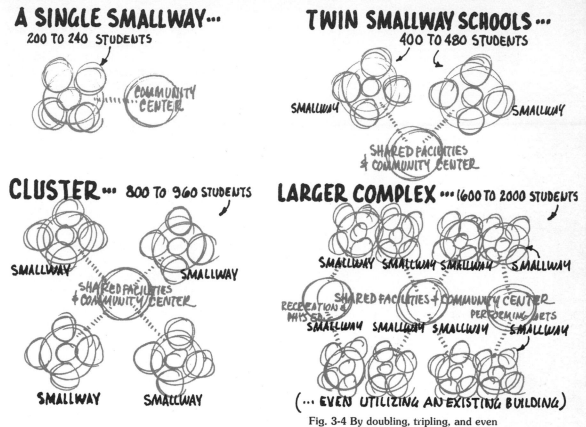

A SINGLE SMALLWAY... 200 TO 240 STUDENTS

COMMUNITY CENTER

TWIN SMALLWAY SCHOOLS... 400 TO 480 STUDENTS

SMALLWAY SMALLWAY

SHARED FACILITIES & COMMUNITY CENTER

CLUSTER... 800 TO 960 STUDENTS

SMALLWAY SMALLWAY

SHARED FACILITIES & COMMUNITY CENTER

SMALLWAY SMALLWAY

LARGER COMPLEX... 1600 TO 2000 STUDENTS

SMALLWAY SMALLWAY SMALLWAY SMALLWAY

RECREATION & PHYS ED. SHARED FACILITIES + COMMUNITY CENTER PERFORMING ARTS

SMALLWAY SMALLWAY SMALLWAY SMALLWAY

(... EVEN UTILIZING AN EXISTING BUILDING)

Fig. 3-4 By doubling, tripling, and even quadrupling the Smallway concept for application to a high school of any size—and at the same time incorporating shared-time facilities with the community—the costs of a small high school can be reduced considerably.

grams, both formal and informal, could distribute these costs over a wider number of people and thereby reduce the unit expense. This is an especially good possibility in the case of library facilities. The community and the school might pool their efforts to set up a joint library, located within the school, that would satisfy the community's needs and at the same time meet the American Library Association's school library standards.

Equipment and materials costs are also reduced if the Smallway plan is adopted as the basis for house plans within larger high schools, since both hardware and software will then be used by all students in the school. See also Fig. 3-4.

PROS AND CONS

A small high school has both disadvantages and advantages. It is up to the administrator to weigh and compare each position.

The Disadvantages

- Since we tend to equate efficiency with large size, there may be a public credibility gap.
- In a small school, kids can't get lost in a crowd. Sometimes the protection of anonymity is useful.
- Smallway can't have large-scale football, cheerleading, and marching bands.
- The school is so small that the failure of any component is clearly visible.
- Resources such as software and audio-visual equipment will be costly in proportion to the number of students.
- Some degree of staff specialization is lost.

The Educational Advantages

- Teachers cannot hide behind the ceremonial system of a large school.
- What students are really like will make a difference.
- Parents can be more deeply involved in a small school. In a large school the power source may be surrounded with a smoke screen of ceremonial systems.
- It costs very little more to be small if the teaching system changes.
- A huge program, based on and tailored to the needs of the students, is feasible.
- At Smallway everyone is needed; no one is left out. All can participate wisely.

CHAPTER 4

HOW TO CREATE TERRITORY FOR LEARNING IN THE SECONDARY SCHOOL

■ ■ ONE OF THE characteristics of our society seems to be that it breeds larger and larger institutions. The reasons for this phenomenon are varied and many. Sometimes sheer size is a direct result of population concentration. In a few cases, large institutions serve social purposes such as racial integration. In others, the often illusory notion of economy of scale may cause the institution to grow to serve great numbers of students. Whatever the reason, large schools continue to represent a significant portion of educational settings in the United States.

One approach to the problem of impersonal size is the development of multischools, in which the sophisticated task of providing an environment in which young people can grow toward adulthood is linked with the specialization potential of the large institution. An enormous monolithic school has little reason for existence. A studied approach to multischools, in which the problems of size from the point of view of the learner are carefully countered, represents a feasible alternative.

Multischools deal with ever-increasing masses of students. Developments in educational and managerial competence, in miniaturization, in electronics, and in understanding individualized education make possible the exploitation of student learning modules within the institution. One of the great tests of managerial skill in the educational field lies in developing semiautonomous units under the umbrella of a larger institution so that individuals may develop a sense of accomplishment by directing their subunits to individual ends with a discrete

TOP: LIBRARY, EVANSTON TOWNSHIP HIGH SCHOOL, EVANSTON, ILL.
BOTTOM: EVANSTON TOWNSHIP HIGH SCHOOL, EVANSTON, ILL.

and unique flavor. A pioneer example has been the Evanston, Illinois, Township High School with its highly developed school-within-a-school organization, evolved under the direction of Lloyd S. Michael.

Developments in technology have broadened the horizons in self-instruction and permit the quick reproduction of material. The great advantages implicit in further development of information retrieval systems and, through miniaturization, the economic possibility of reproducing expensive equipment at many locations make more complex learning environments viable. As the computer becomes more sophisticated, it will continue to be reduced in size and perhaps in cost. This will make such equipment more widely available for individual responses in the learning process.

In dealing with disadvantaged students, the impermanence of a constantly shifting organization or the impersonality of large-class instruction is contraindicated. Success generally comes in places where individuals really communicate with individuals. Small groups, close contact, careful follow-up, patience, and individualized programs are factors that work.

In the multischool teachers must be sympathetic to the task, believing in and liking what they are doing. This requirement goes far beyond selecting the right teacher. Most teachers begin the task full of idealism and enthusiasm. The system allows them to lose their enthusiasm or lets it wear away.

Think of the fascinating study in which teachers were told privately, but quite inaccurately, that the children in their classes really were underachievers with very high IQs. The teachers then succeeded in getting ordinary children to perform on an amazingly high level.

Then, too, the faculty should be coddled and cared for, provided with planning space, aides, soft music, and carpeting, kept from getting overtired, frequently stimulated intellectually, frequently injected with enthusiasm, and frequently given the soul-warming experiences of success. Teaching is a tough job, and teachers need all the fringe benefits that a lower-echelon business executive accepts as a matter of course, except perhaps the three-martini, two-hour lunch hour.

The focus on problem solving in the multischool should be direct and not rely on transfer of learning. If the student cannot communicate adequately, he should be placed in a situation in which it is important, if not critical, to him to communicate well. It really does not do to suggest that Latin, in the long haul, is the real answer.

Whenever schools have anything important to do, a multigraded enterprise that re-creates itself has been developed to sustain the process. Teams and bands and newspapers thrive on a mix of experienced and inexperienced participants, with the older hands initiating the younger ones until the less experienced can take over. Probably, if learning were ever considered to be important, the same kind of system as that of the football team would be used, along with the whole hierarchy of coaches, aides, trainees, and student managers.

Variety is a way of life (see Fig. 4-1). In schools, this has not been true in an institutional sense, although some teachers have had to vary their approaches or face death by atrophy. The lovely line about the British civil service—"These plants are the better for periodic repotting"—has a clear meaning for schools.

Learning takes place best in the midst of a conflict of ideas. It can be argued that the best schools are those in which children's heads and brains move from idea to idea like spectators at a tennis match until the children cannot resist getting deeply involved in the argument. The sharpening of minds that takes place under controlled bull-session arrangements is of real importance.

Independent work at the secondary school level takes place best in small groups. There are few real loners at this age, and most students sharpen their wits in small-group conversation, reinforcing each other in the process of learning. But variety in itself is good; what works well one day may not work the next.

Particularly in schools dealing with a wide mix of students, the mix of the facilities may add a creative note to the environment (see Fig. 4-2). There is no particularly solemn need for all the teachers of English to be together and for all the vocational offerings to be located behind the boiler room or for the guidance staff to set up a pseudopsychiatric clinic near the administrative space. A mix of activities and people may provide stimulus to the program and to each other. Most of the inherent difficulties are details.

A school should provide a sense of identity, an awareness of high stimulation, and a warmth of security to all its students. These matters of atmosphere and emotion are basic ingredients for learning. Disadvantaged children are truly disadvantaged in these areas and need most desperately to catch up in their emotional stock before learning becomes too critical a task.

MULTISCHOOL: A SECONDARY SCHOOL DESIGN IN RESPONSE TO TODAY'S NEEDS

If students are going to be deeply involved in learning, they need a place in which to learn. Classrooms are

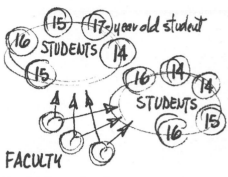

Fig. 4-1 Variety benefits both students and faculty.

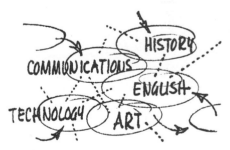

Fig. 4-2 Mixture of people and activities.

spaces in which teachers can be involved. Schools need some. They more often need a place where four or five students can work for extended times on a problem that is of significance both to them and to the school. This school proposes that students have such a space, called their "turf," and that it be recognized as the place where much of their learning occurs. The turf provides space for generalized learning, but as students follow individual interests and areas of specialization, they will be redeployed with others of similar interest for part of the time.

One critical path (see Fig. 4-3) illustrates in a generalized way parallel activities of student groups in both nonspecialized and specialized areas. A student, as at present, will be involved in a number of critical paths at one time; some in skill areas and others in history and English or other basic educational areas that form a common part of student experience.

In reviewing the critical path chart, note that students receive some generalized information on a topic in large-group presentations but that most of their effort is spent in an in-depth study of a problem that illuminates a topic. The school focuses on inquiry, process, and problem solving. Skills and facts are learned. More often these are learned in the context of problems so that mastering skills and facts becomes important, not because students are told to learn, but because they need the facts or skills to get the job done, to do their share of the work in small student task forces, and to help solve the problem.

Using an analogy, Lewis Yoho of the University of Indiana contends that in most subjects students in effect should learn to pitch and bat and run and slide and know the rules of baseball. But these skills and facts should not

Fig. 4-3 Critical path chart.

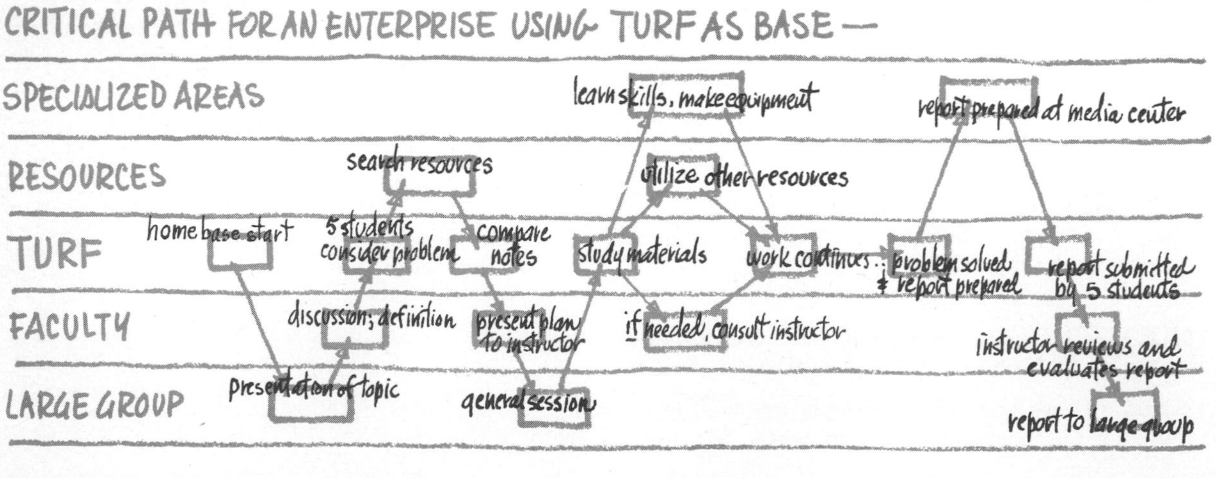

CRITICAL PATH FOR AN ENTERPRISE USING TURF AS BASE —

SPECIALIZED AREAS — learn skills, make equipment — report prepared at media center

RESOURCES — search resources — utilize other resources

TURF — home base start — 5 students consider problem — compare notes — study materials — work continues — problem solved & report prepared — report submitted by 5 students

FACULTY — discussion; definition — present plan to instructor — if needed, consult instructor — instructor reviews and evaluates report

LARGE GROUP — presentation of topic — general session — report to large group

be learned without ever playing a game of baseball. When this happens, the skills and facts are abstract and theoretical and lack meaning. Most schools never really put the students into a ball game. This great occasion apparently will occur only at graduate school level. How much better it would be to put the students into a game so that needed skills and facts have meaning. Using problems that illuminate topics in any field, students can learn to solve the problems (that is, to think) and can, in the light of judiciously selected problems, understand the need for and learn more effectively the skills and facts necessary to do the job.

As schools grow larger, the smallest subunit of the school grows in importance. Learning is the task of the student; the turf he shares with three or four other students is his major work area (see Fig. 4-4). This home base is also a schedule base since it is used for all learning that does not require the student to move outside his learning cluster for specialties of staff or equipment. The turf can be outfitted to suit the task at hand, for science, for design, or for study or discussion. It has the capability of infinite individualization.

The instructor serves as a counselor for learning and as a guide and critic of the thinking procedures of students. If a task is to be accomplished, an important checkpoint is the review of the plan of attack. Here five students and a faculty member critically analyze the definition of the problem, the method of attack, the resources needed, the time required, and the evaluation proposed. Similarly, the evaluation of the success of the inquiry should be revealing and illuminating to students as well as to the staff.

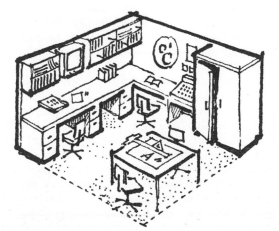

Fig. 4-4 Nonspecialized home base for five students.

Fig. 4-5 A cluster (100 students).

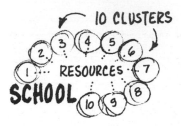

Fig. 4-6 A school (ten clusters).

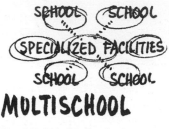

Fig. 4-7 A multischool.

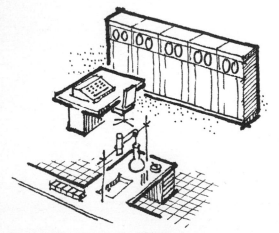

Fig. 4-8 Shared specialized facilities.

Twenty turfs make up a "cluster" of 100 students. A group of ten clusters is formed into a school of 1,000 students with its administration devoted to improving instruction and to aiding staff and students. A series of schools forms a "multischool," in which the overall organization supports the operations of its component parts, provides services and resources, and diverts interrupting demands upon the schools. See Figs. 4-5, 4-6, and 4-7.

Supporting the clusters and the schools are specialized areas offering experiences in the world of work, in specialized scientific inquiry, in the arts, in skills of communication, and in physical activity (see Fig. 4-8).

If the strategy is to involve students and staff, one of the major tactics is the creative use of a wide variety of media in the learning process. The rare quality of a stimulating resource center comes into being when man's communication resources, his varied languages, provide material as a basis for student learning. The resource center has books of all kinds in quantities not dreamed of ten years ago. It overflows with tapes and films and microfilms and closed-circuit television and retrieval systems.

The strategy is involvement. This applies to the faculty as well as to the students. The faculty team for a cluster will have a heartening breadth of experience and variety of outlook. Planning together for students in order to see the process of education more clearly will be a major function of the staff. Planning with students for their more perceptive involvement in the study of issues will be a joint staff-student process. Student planning and attacking issues are central to the learning process. The student team undertaking these incursions may well, for the most part, be based on the turf group. At times, this group could be five tenth graders involved in a search for truth in a social studies area. At other times, it could be an ungraded group focusing on a skill area. At still other times, an enterprise could be established.

An enterprise is essentially a long-term project of some scope that moves from idea to plan to execution to evaluation and then continues in operational cycles for some time. Frequently, an enterprise involves both experienced and inexperienced students. As a result the less experienced become more experienced or more knowledgeable. Periodically, the enterprise is broken down, overhauled, and reconstituted. The enterprise is a central tactic going far beyond a team-teaching approach into the area of a student team inquiry approach. As the multischool has experience with enterprises (a simulation in business education or a sociological research project in social studies or a writing project in English, to cite a few examples), it will use this tactic a great deal. It will vary the composition of the enterprise, use the device to help disadvantaged kids get over their blocks by the example and the help of more experienced students, and in general be creative in the deployment of a device that has been shown to have high utility.

THE TURF CONCEPT

The basic unit of the school is a turf designed for five students. This will serve as home base, study area, problem-solving area, and learning space and, in fact, provide space for learning. When specialized facilities or staff are needed, the student moves to the appropriate areas in the school for a part of the day.

During the course of the day, a student may spend 50 percent of his time in the turf. Of the five students, two or three usually will be in the turf at one time. The turf should store books, media, materials, and outer clothing and provide work space for reading in English, for writing and research in history, for calculation in mathematics, and for some general science operations. The members of the turf should be able to outfit their space in accordance with their needs and to draw from storage the things necessary to support their tasks. A bit of individualizing the turf won't hurt either, but borrowing the sign for the principal's office likely will be regarded as gilding the lily.

The students in a turf may be drawn from a common grade level or from four grade levels. They may be a mix of leader and follower or all one kind of student. The sexes could be mixed at one time and separated the next

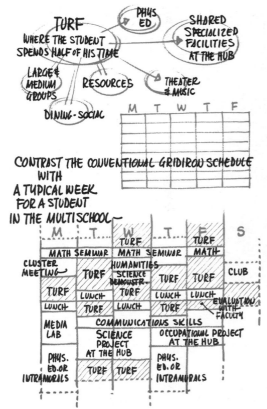

Fig. 4-9 Conventional schedule compared with that in a multischool.

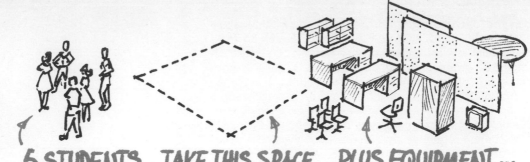

5 STUDENTS...TAKE THIS SPACE... PLUS EQUIPMENT...
(sometimes of varying ages) (12'x12' = 144 sq.feet) (appropriate for their own special programs)

AND CREATE THEIR OWN TURF...
A TERRITORY FOR LEARNING

THIS TURF IS HOME BASE
FOR ALL FIVE STUDENTS ....
BUT DURING THE DAY, AT ANY HOUR,
ONLY 2 OR 3 STUDENTS
WILL BE WORKING HERE ➝

WHILE THE OTHER 2 OR 3 ARE
AT THE SHARED FACILITIES, OR IN
LARGE OR MEDIUM GROUP SPACES.

DURING THE DAY, MANY LEARNING ACTIVITIES
WILL OCCUR IN THE TURF —
INVOLVING DIFFERENT
COMBINATIONS OF STUDENTS,
FACULTY, MEDIA AND MATERIALS.

READING
WRITING
DRAWING

BASIC SCIENCE EXPERIMENTS, REPORTS,
CONSTRUCTION OF MODELS, DEVICES, MATERIALS.

COMPUTER ASSISTED INSTRUCTION
DIAL ACCESS LISTENING AND VIEWING
TEACHING MACHINE INSTRUCTION
TELEVISION INSTRUCTION

DISCUSSION WITH OTHER STUDENTS
OR FACULTY. SMALL SEMINARS,
COUNSELLING & GUIDANCE.

Fig. 4-10 Learning activities within the turf.

GIVE FIVE STUDENTS THEIR OWN TURF—

CHANGEABLE TERRITORY FOR LEARNING— NEAR RESOURCES & FACULTY

HERE ARE SOME OF THE WAYS THEY CAN USE IT ....

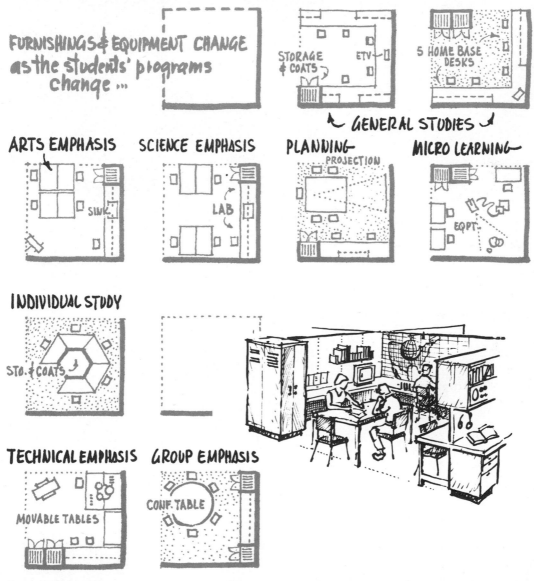

FURNISHINGS & EQUIPMENT CHANGE as the students' programs change ...

STORAGE & COATS

ETV

5 HOME BASE DESKS

GENERAL STUDIES

ARTS EMPHASIS

SINK

SCIENCE EMPHASIS

LAB

PLANNING

PROJECTION

MICRO LEARNING

EQPT.

INDIVIDUAL STUDY

STO. & COATS

TECHNICAL EMPHASIS

MOVABLE TABLES

GROUP EMPHASIS

CONF. TABLE

Fig. 4-11 Flexibility of the turf.

time. Without overdoing the fluidity, students and staff should redeploy themselves deliberately from time to time for observable ends. This is no random pattern but is purposely complex, tailored to the special needs of each individual student. The computer helps in scheduling. See Figs. 4-9, 4-10, and 4-11.

COMBINING TWENTY TURFS AND A FACULTY TEAM TO CREATE A CLUSTER OF 100 STUDENTS

Twenty turfs make a cluster of 100 students with a staff assigned to the cluster and responsible for a fair share of the student's learning (see Figs. 4-12 and 4-13). The staff's composition relates to the ways in which the work of a group of 100 students can best be advanced. One deployment of staff might be the following:

Fig. 4-12 A faculty-and-student cluster.

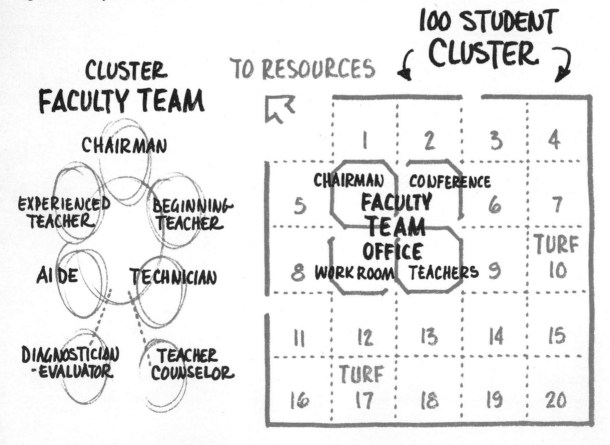

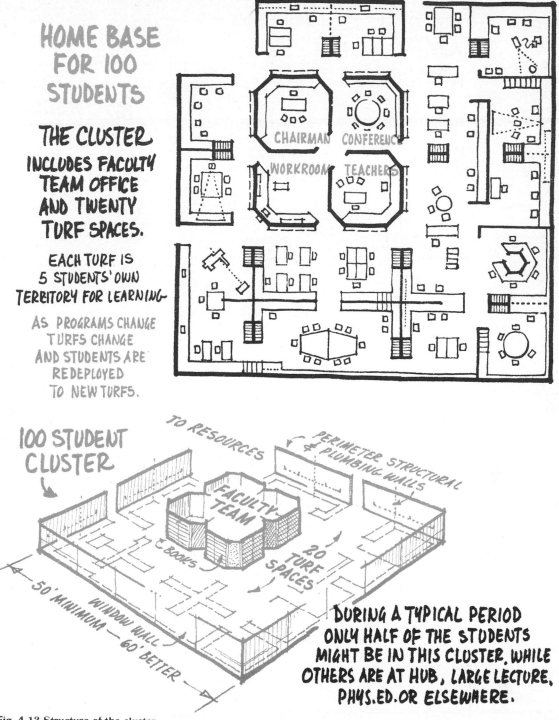

HOME BASE FOR 100 STUDENTS

THE CLUSTER INCLUDES FACULTY TEAM OFFICE AND TWENTY TURF SPACES.

EACH TURF IS 5 STUDENTS' OWN TERRITORY FOR LEARNING

AS PROGRAMS CHANGE TURFS CHANGE AND STUDENTS ARE REDEPLOYED TO NEW TURFS.

CHAIRMAN   CONFERENCE
WORKROOM   TEACHERS

100 STUDENT CLUSTER

TO RESOURCES

PERIMETER STRUCTURAL & PLUMBING WALLS

FACULTY TEAM

BOOKS

20 TURF SPACES

50' MINIMUM — 60' BETTER

WINDOW WALL

DURING A TYPICAL PERIOD ONLY HALF OF THE STUDENTS MIGHT BE IN THIS CLUSTER, WHILE OTHERS ARE AT HUB, LARGE LECTURE, PHYS. ED. OR ELSEWHERE.

Fig. 4-13 Structure of the cluster.

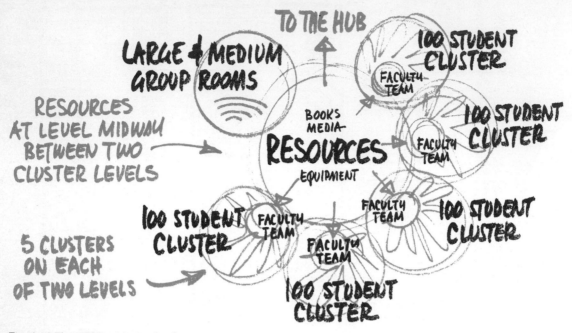

TO THE HUB

LARGE & MEDIUM GROUP ROOMS

100 STUDENT CLUSTER

FACULTY TEAM

RESOURCES AT LEVEL MIDWAY BETWEEN TWO CLUSTER LEVELS

BOOKS MEDIA

RESOURCES

EQUIPMENT

FACULTY TEAM

100 STUDENT CLUSTER

100 STUDENT CLUSTER

FACULTY TEAM

FACULTY TEAM

100 STUDENT CLUSTER

5 CLUSTERS ON EACH OF TWO LEVELS

FACULTY TEAM

100 STUDENT CLUSTER

Fig. 4-14 The 1,000-student school.

1. Chairman, a high-level professional teacher.

2. Two teachers, one of them a beginning teacher, whose jobs are planning the educational program, advising students in problem solving, presenting conflicts, counseling in the learning process, and serving as resource people.

3. Two aide-technicians to keep matters moving, find needed materials, provide elements of direction to students under the supervision of teachers, and make sure that what is needed to learn is there and is in good working order. Aides and technicians could be parents or volunteers. The reeducation of parents is a useful by-product.

4. A diagnostician-evaluator: Available to several clusters, this staff member would regularly review the position in which students are and their needs to get where they are going. This involves individual work, supervision, seeing that work is done, prescription, evaluating the prescription, and repeating these assignments as needed.

5. Teacher counselor, a member of the group staff, perhaps shared by two clusters but, it is hoped, in times or in areas of need belonging to the individual cluster staff. The counselor's task is to see the whole student,

help with vocational needs, point out further educational needs, know homes, and keep in touch with social agencies. Even with the increased mobility of students, by using a four-year cluster the counselor has relatively few students to get to know each year. The counselor is a part of the staff group dealing with the cluster students and does not have an isolated, ivory-tower guidance approach to students.

PUTTING TEN CLUSTERS AROUND RESOURCES TO FORM A 1,000-STUDENT SCHOOL

Ten clusters brought together around central resources form a school (see Figs. 4-14, 4-15, and 4-16). The school will contain a large-group meeting space, seating a cluster at a time, some medium-size spaces for twenty or so students at a time, and, a major requirement, free access to resources. The 1,000-student school will also have its own dining and social space, administration, and student activities. The space pattern of each cluster in the school follows:

1. Infrequently the entire cluster will meet to start an area of work, to plan, and to evaluate what has been done.

2. Occasionally a group of twenty students will plan with an adult in deciding on an attack on a problem, in evaluating progress, and in getting past a sticky point.

3. Most of the time, three to five students will be involved with materials drawn to provide information or skills to solve a problem. The group will require work space, storage for its materials, typewriters, and access to resources, books, tapes, a computer, science equipment, and so on. Once in a while, a student will handle a problem in depth on his or her own. The student should be able to share the turf with his or her colleagues to get that task done.

4. The staff will spend most of its time in work with the groups of two to five students, either at their turf or in a conference room or faculty office.

The required spaces thus are:

Fig. 4-15 A cross section of a ten-cluster school.

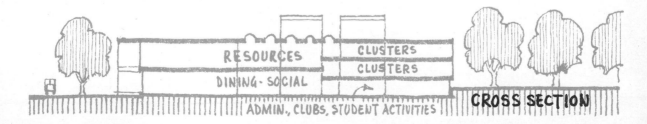

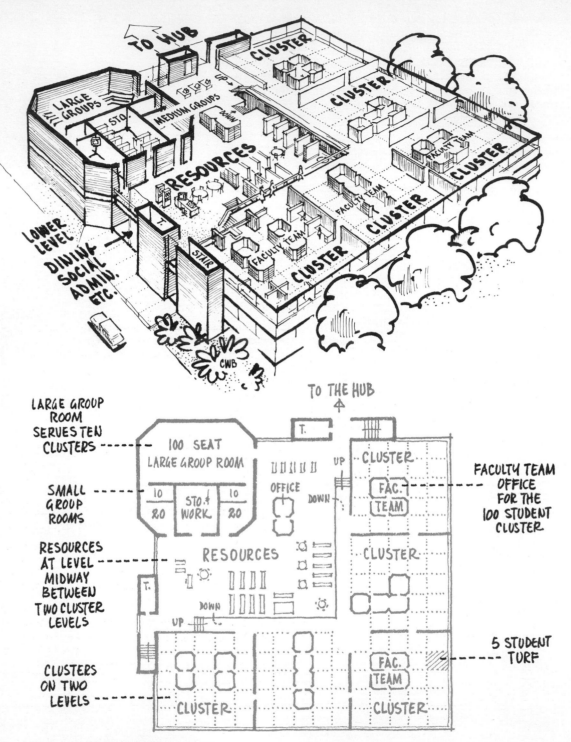

Fig. 4-16 Structure of the ten-cluster school.

1. A shared 100-plus student large-group room designed for group interaction. Lectures have been discarded in favor of written or taped information transmission.

2. Two twenty-plus student seminar rooms.

3. Work space, turf, near or in the midst of resources, broken by students into simple subgroupings, usually five students (two or three of them at their turf at any one time). Storage is required.

4. Faculty team space in the clusters.

5. Dining-social space; school administration office.

THE NEED FOR SPECIALIZED FACILITIES AT A CENTRAL HUB

Specialized Clusters

The way in which student time modules develop will depend upon the needs of students as an expert staff has determined them in consultation with the students. Thus, there should be room for variation in the use of spaces. This is not an efficient procedure in terms of utilization but perhaps a more efficient procedure in terms of learning. See Figs. 4-17, 4-18, 4-19, and 4-20.

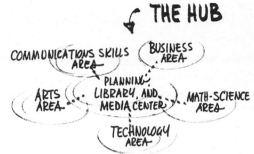

Fig. 4-17 The hub of the school.

Fig. 4-18 Planning, library, and media center.

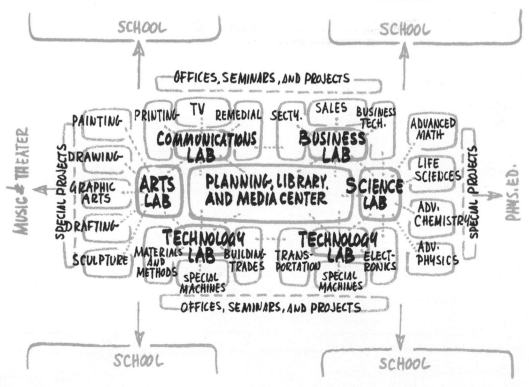

FOR EXPERIENCE IN THE WORLD OF WORK 100 STUDENTS PROGRAM, DESIGN, PRODUCE, AND DISTRIBUTE AN AM-FM RADIO –

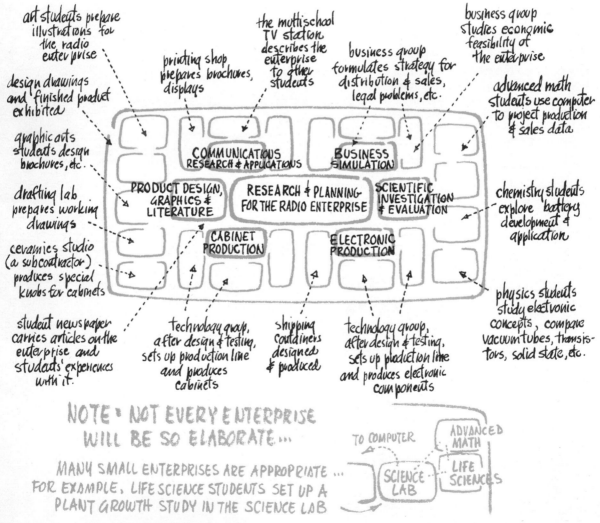

art students prepare illustrations for the radio enterprise

design drawings and finished product exhibited

graphic arts students design brochures, etc.

drafting lab prepares working drawings

ceramics studio (a subcontractor) produces special knobs for cabinets

student newspaper carries articles on the enterprise and students' experiences with it.

printing shop prepares brochures, displays

the multischool TV station describes the enterprise to other students

business group formulates strategy for distribution & sales, legal problems, etc.

business group studies economic feasibility of the enterprise

advanced math students use computer to project production & sales data

chemistry students explore battery development & application

physics students study electronic concepts, compare vacuum tubes, transistors, solid state, etc.

COMMUNICATIONS RESEARCH & APPLICATIONS

BUSINESS SIMULATION

PRODUCT DESIGN, GRAPHICS & LITERATURE

RESEARCH & PLANNING FOR THE RADIO ENTERPRISE

SCIENTIFIC INVESTIGATION & EVALUATION

CABINET PRODUCTION

ELECTRONIC PRODUCTION

technology group, after design & testing, sets up production line and produces cabinets

shipping containers designed & produced

technology group, after design & testing, sets up production line and produces electronic components

NOTE: NOT EVERY ENTERPRISE WILL BE SO ELABORATE...

MANY SMALL ENTERPRISES ARE APPROPRIATE... FOR EXAMPLE, LIFE SCIENCE STUDENTS SET UP A PLANT GROWTH STUDY IN THE SCIENCE LAB

TO COMPUTER

ADVANCED MATH

SCIENCE LAB

LIFE SCIENCES

Fig. 4-19 An enterprise being executed at the hub.

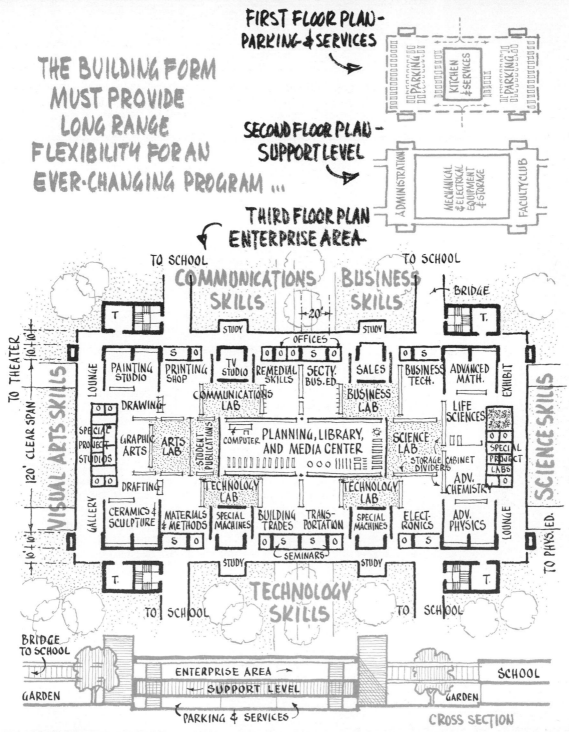

Fig. 4-20 Building-form flexibility.

Mathematics-Science Area

In science, the problem-solving approach inherent in many of the newer programs will be enhanced by emphasis upon small-group student teams attacking different problems that depend on the interest, capability, or level of mathematics of the five-person teams. In outline, a small amount of time may be devoted to presentation and general theory. A great deal of time will be spent by student teams of three to five students seeking solutions to problems developed by them with faculty aid and so arranged that the major problems tackled will cover the major ideas involved in the subject area. The science facilities will require easy access to the library, space for the student team to deliberate, laboratory space to test the hypotheses developed, a highly developed self-service storage and dispensing area, and access to single-concept films that will do much of the skill training.

This kind of open laboratory requires that faculty be available on a consulting basis. Aides will be needed.

Communications Skills Area

Reading, writing, speaking, and grammar can be involved in a communications skills center. The diagnostic level will stress repeated evaluation and new prescription of helpful practice. The center can operate with heavy dependence upon tape recorders, availability of tapes, need for single-concept training films, videotapes, and programmed instruction.   .

In the same area there should be developed a communications skills shop area in which the skills are reinforced by use with varying media. Poetry or short stories written in the communications skills area can be printed in the communications shop, or poetry can be read and taped, plays performed or videotaped, or posters made. The use of today's media to reinforce training in the use of words is perhaps not good McLuhan, but it is good education.

Technology Area (Technical, Vocational, Occupational)

Here, too, the major emphasis should be on problem solving, such as designing, producing, packaging, and making economic studies of the connectors for a space frame. The skills of design and production are learned in the context of dealing with the central problem. When a team of students has set up a production line or an enterprise, younger, less experienced students can be introduced into the enterprise. In time, someone will create a new design, reworking the production line, improving the product, and reducing its cost.

In this kind of cluster, the technology laboratory serves as the inquiry center for the technology area, while the development of more highly specialized skills clusters about the central motif.

Business Area

Skills training is important for business, but it should be learned in the context of the needs of American business. The American business laboratory is a process-centered work space where the problems of various industries and businesses are simulated. Students must work in small teams at solving the problems, using the skill-training laboratories to develop the skills that are shown by simulation to have value.

The use of computers for simulation experiences in business will be as important as is learning the language of computers as a vocational skill.

Arts Area

Clusters are implied in the arts, music, the home arts, and drama. In this school, the development of an ivory tower for the arts is avoided. The arts are expected to draw sustenance from literature and philosophy and the ongoing operations of the school. Their showplace is Main Street in the school. The arts should be mixed with the general and specialized activities of the school so that design is important in the communications shop, in home arts, and in vocational and occupational areas.

Generalized Spaces Library

The library is a pervasive space mixed with clusters, extending and ranging through the school. Its card catalog is a computer print-out available anywhere and no longer restricting the design of the library. Its electronic nerves allow dialing from any location to a central tape bank, where audio and video signals can be secured to serve the educational process. The book collection requirement is manyfold greater than a textbook system, for readings are collected, research is processed, and resources with wide-ranging areas of interest are a prerequisite for the program.

Faculty, Administration, Counseling, and Guidance

The needs for space for consulting with students and for

planning have been stressed in the clusters. The same ideas apply to all kinds of clusters. A faculty club for the school as a whole, not unlike the New Trier West Faculty Club, is required not only for what it does to prove to the faculty the importance of their work but for its provision of a bridge to the community. Many of the increased numbers of meetings with community leaders and parents can take place here, at lunch or breakfast or whenever people can come. In many respects, the faculty club could be a major community service space, reducing the isolation of the staff.

The administrative space in such a secondary school is modest and is devoted to stimulating and supporting the clusters. It will be a staff and community space. Frequent meetings with members of the community will be held to assure that the two forces are working together for the children. The school must understand its community and the needs of its students, and members of the community, along with the students, must grow in competence to deal with the larger world.

Traditional student activities will tend to be reduced in this kind of school since, in a sense, most of the club activities will be incorporated in the student workday. Student social activities should be planned and developed by the clusters or schools of the multischool. The availability of a group of schools in the larger organization gives these a key role in the student activity programs and in the possibility of intramural programs. School publications on a school basis will provide greater opportunities for students than would a monolithic organization.

ASSEMBLING ALL THE COMPONENTS TO CREATE THE 4,000-STUDENT MULTISCHOOL

Four 1,000-student schools, together with the specialized clusters and services, could make up a multischool (see Figs. 4-21 and 4-22). Its reasons for existence lie in the nature of the modern secondary school and the society in which it finds itself. The sheer cost of specialization and the increasing need for kinds of specialization in part of the school life of each student, together with the great increase in the variety of knowledge and skills, make a larger unit almost unavoidable. Then, too, with the increased concentration of population, the sheer physical problem of providing a host of small units becomes overpowering.

The larger secondary school focused on the smallest component, the turf, offers a way to meet the conflicting needs of individualization and mass. Certainly, in this process the sophistication of the administrator and the capabilities of the communications systems, human and mechanical, are major factors in success or failure.

THE MULTISCHOOL AS THE FOCAL POINT FOR URBAN LIFE

In dealing with the disadvantaged blacks in America's center cities, the bloom is off Nicely-Nicely, and the specter of black power is raised as a serious alternative. The argument is advanced that since the country does not seem to be able to mount a consistent, vigorous, and instantly successful program to resolve poverty and color problems, the answer lies in withdrawing from the white society, cultivating power, and ultimately rejoining the struggle when a proved power system has been developed.

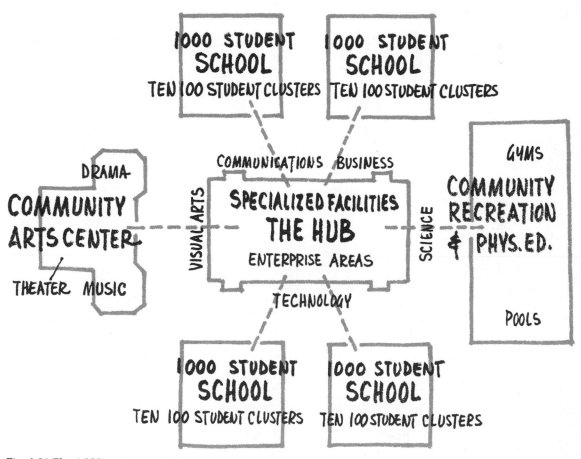

Fig. 4-21 The 4,000-student multischool.

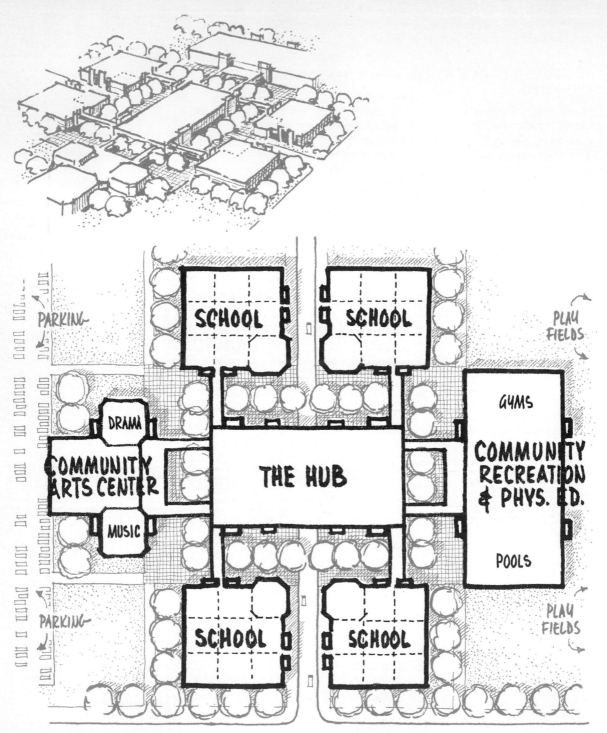

Fig. 4-22 A garden court school.

This is reverse apartheid. It is a kind of alienation that springs from deep despair on the part of the deprived, the apathy of the larger American public, and, no doubt, a certain amount of opportunism on all sides.

The schools are in this situation to the hilt. The slightly dressed-up business-as-usual approach doesn't work. There is heavy pressure toward decentralization, which is often looked upon as an antischool movement in which parents and community leaders in the slums are about to take over the control of the schools. That this has been a recognized pattern in affluent suburbs is not introduced into the conversation and is ignored. The center city multischool has a major task on its hands which, if it is bungled, will add greatly to the forces of alienation and withdrawal apartheid.

The following notions try to relate the school outlined here to the center city and its problems.

1. An inquiry-centered school will do better in the slums of America because its program is not primarily an accretion of facts and attitudes, much of which is learned in the community and home environment in the more affluent areas. The program is less ceremonial and abstract. The inquiry school emphasizes a process that can be understood at many levels and that has a more meaningful and concrete goal. You don't learn something because someone says it is good for you and you will need it one day (this is often untrue). You learn because you need the skill or the fact today.

2. An enterprise school that mixes leader and follower, experienced and inexperienced, profits from the fact that the one who teaches learns a great deal. One of the major discoveries of the efforts to improve education in the white or black ghettos of poverty has been that if an older deprived child helps a younger deprived child to learn to read, they both improve a good deal. They communicate, and they work together without fear or division.

3. If there is one thing that is needed in the center city school, it is a faculty that cares.

4. The faculty and the parents must and can work together for the good of the children. This cooperation happens elsewhere. Given the urge and support, it can happen in the usual slum school. We cannot continue to staff so many of the ghetto schools with people who are limited in outlook and broken in spirit, who look upon the parents and children as far down in the pecking order.

5. Without renouncing its demand for the best work the student can produce, the school has a responsibility to vary its offering or its approaches so that what is expected of the student both is within his capability and seems rational to him. Much of the middle-class school

NOTE SOME OF THE SPECIAL PROBLEMS ENCOUNTERED WHEN BUILDING IN THE CITY —

... NEW FORMS FOR URBAN SCHOOLS ARE NEEDED.

* SITES ARE SMALL ... LAND IS EXPENSIVE ... URBAN BUILDING FORMS (COMPACT, MULTI LEVEL) ARE MOST APPROPRIATE ...

* THE URBAN SCHOOL (STRONGLY INFLUENCED BY NEIGHBORS) IS BEST WHEN INTEGRATED WITH THE TOTAL URBAN ENVIRONMENT, WITH OTHER CULTURAL & EDUCATIONAL AGENCIES ...

COMMERCE · RECREATION & PARKS · CULTURAL CENTER · MULTI-SCHOOL · INDUSTRY · GOVERNMENT · COMMUNITY COLLEGE

* AIR RIGHTS DEVELOPMENT IS NOW AN OPPORTUNITY FOR PRIME LOCATION, GOOD ACCESS, SPACE, DRAMA ...

EXPRESSWAY

* WHERE LAND IS VERY EXPENSIVE THE HIGH-RISE SCHOOL MAY BE APPROPRIATE ...

* NEXT — SCHOOLS WILL SHARE MULTIUSE STRUCTURES WITH OTHER TENANTS

Fig. 4-23 Creating new forms for city schools.

IN THE CITY, PLAN THE MULTISCHOOL WITH OTHER EDUCATIONAL, CULTURAL, AND COMMUNITY FACILITIES

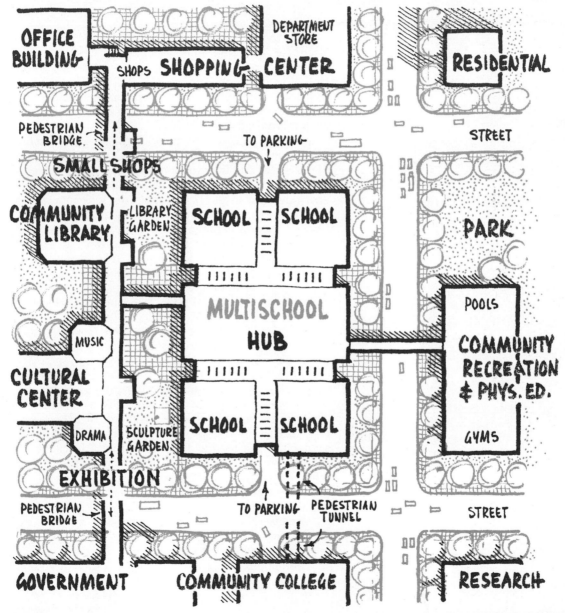

Fig. 4-24 The urban multischool.

program is a ceremonial system that lacks real meaning but is accepted by the middle-class society and therefore does no great harm. It is irrational to the disadvantaged child and should not be imposed upon him.

6. The rich variety of media may, with major exposure of disadvantaged students to it, be more effective than the stereotyped textbook approach. It will take mountains of materials, helpful adults, and enthusiastic teaching to put the media to work.

Tape recorders instead of pencils, adding machines, electronic recording and viewing devices instead of books, pictures, sounds, then words—this may be the kind of emphasis and progression necessary before some of the children come out of the darkness in which they find themselves. If the school does not move boldly, it will keep these children in darkness.

In planning a new urban school, the uses of the school must be thought through carefully, as we have suggested, to make sure that the program leads the design instead of following it. You may find that you don't really need a new school after all. The school you seek may be the middle three floors in a new office building. It may share facilities with an existing school or utilize a conveniently located old warehouse. It may be no more than some office space where the logistics for sending students to school throughout the city are controlled.

In urban areas, where land values continue to rise in what appears to be an irreversible trend, the concept of joint occupancy deserves attention. The idea of combining schools with other public functions or linking them with housing or commercial space is not new, but it has not been widely explored.

As the Educational Facilities Laboratories has pointed out, the first reason for developing a joint-occupancy effort is obvious: money. Not only is it difficult to put aside city sites for schools, it is also self-defeating because it creates a dwindling property tax base. By placing a school in a high-rise building, for example, the city retains its tax base of revenue-producing properties, permits high-rise occupants to have a neighborhood school, and produces some unusual educational experiences for the students involved.

Whatever the school is and wherever it is, the staff should give a high priority to organizing the process of involving many people in planning and decision making. The best approach is to designate as a planning cadre the group that ultimately will operate the school. A steering committee from the faculty should be selected. This committee should include a cross section of the staff—people with optimistic but not necessarily similar views, people

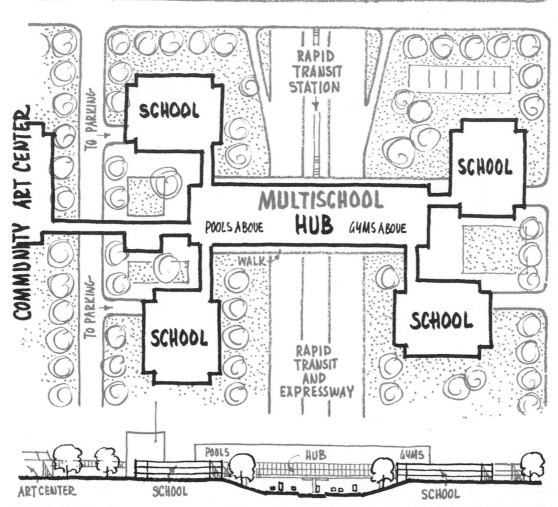

Fig. 4-25 Building along and over expressways.

IN THE CITY, WHEN LAND IS VERY EXPENSIVE STACK THE COMPONENTS TO CREATE A HIGH·RISE MULTISCHOOL

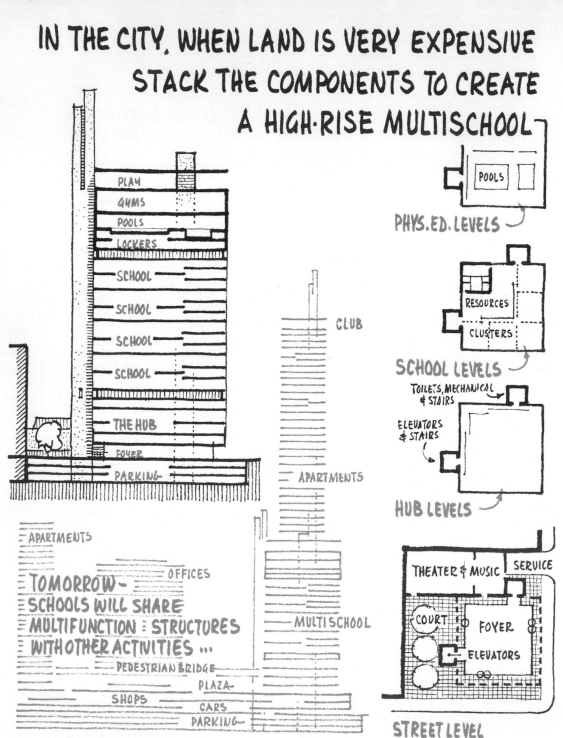

PLAY
GYMS
POOLS
LOCKERS
SCHOOL
SCHOOL
SCHOOL
SCHOOL
THE HUB
FOYER
PARKING

CLUB
APARTMENTS

APARTMENTS
OFFICES

TOMORROW —
SCHOOLS WILL SHARE
MULTIFUNCTION STRUCTURES
WITH OTHER ACTIVITIES ...

MULTISCHOOL

PEDESTRIAN BRIDGE
PLAZA
SHOPS
CARS
PARKING

POOLS
PHYS. ED. LEVELS

RESOURCES
CLUSTERS
SCHOOL LEVELS

TOILETS, MECHANICAL & STAIRS
ELEVATORS & STAIRS
HUB LEVELS

THEATER & MUSIC   SERVICE
COURT   FOYER
ELEVATORS
STREET LEVEL

Fig. 4-26 The high-rise multischool.

IN THE METROPOLITAN REGION
CALCULATED INTERDEPENDENCE* WILL LINK
MULTISCHOOLS AND OTHER FACILITIES—

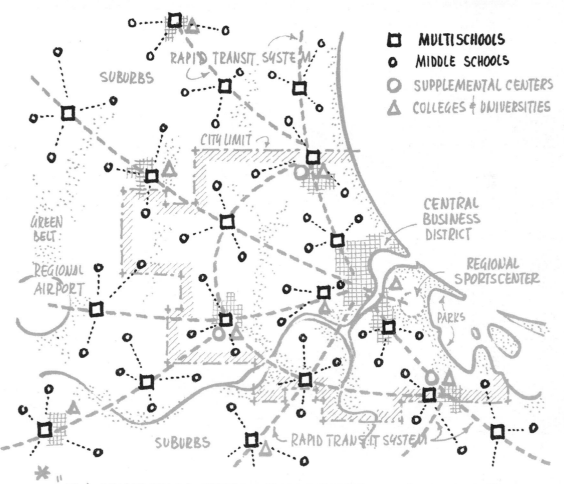

Legend:
- ☐ MULTISCHOOLS
- ● MIDDLE SCHOOLS
- ⬡ SUPPLEMENTAL CENTERS
- △ COLLEGES & UNIVERSITIES

RAPID TRANSIT SYSTEM
SUBURBS
CITY LIMIT
GREEN BELT
REGIONAL AIRPORT
CENTRAL BUSINESS DISTRICT
REGIONAL SPORTS CENTER
PARKS
SUBURBS
RAPID TRANSIT SYSTEM

*"IF A SINGLE TREND STANDS OUT MOST CLEARLY AS A DEVELOPMENT OF PRESENT TIMES, IT IS PROBABLY THE CONDITION WHICH SOMEONE HAS CHARACTERIZED AS "CALCULATED INTERDEPENDENCE." NO AGENCY OR INDIVIDUAL OPERATES ALONE OR INDEPENDENTLY ANY LONGER. THE KEYNOTE IN SOCIAL PROGRESS LIES, IN FACT, IN SUCCESSFULLY RELATING INDIVIDUAL EFFORTS TO MUTUAL OR OVERLAPPING INTERESTS."
— from "Emerging Library Systems" — The University of the State of New York, Feb., '67

Fig. 4-27 The relation of the urban multischool to other facilities.

EXISTING SCHOOL
CLASSROOM BOXES
ALONG A LONG CORRIDOR

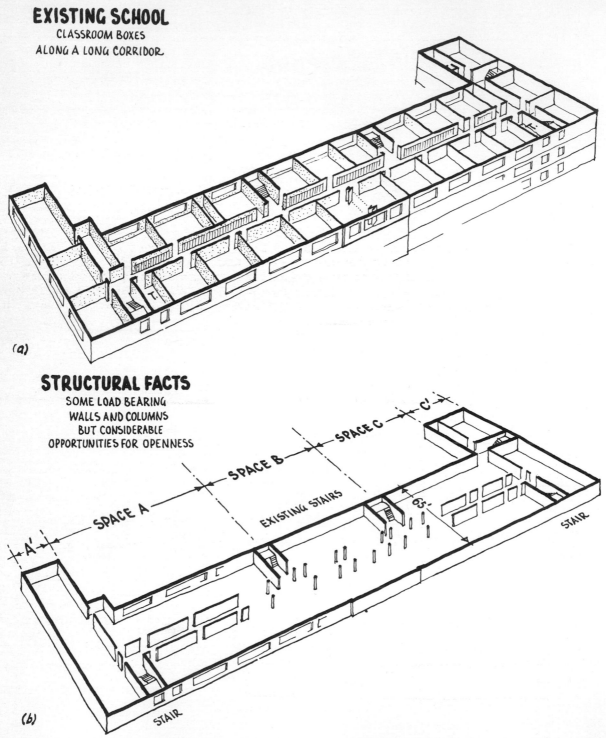

(a)

STRUCTURAL FACTS
SOME LOAD BEARING
WALLS AND COLUMNS
BUT CONSIDERABLE
OPPORTUNITIES FOR OPENNESS

SPACE A

SPACE B

SPACE C

C'

65'

EXISTING STAIRS

STAIR

A'

STAIR

(b)

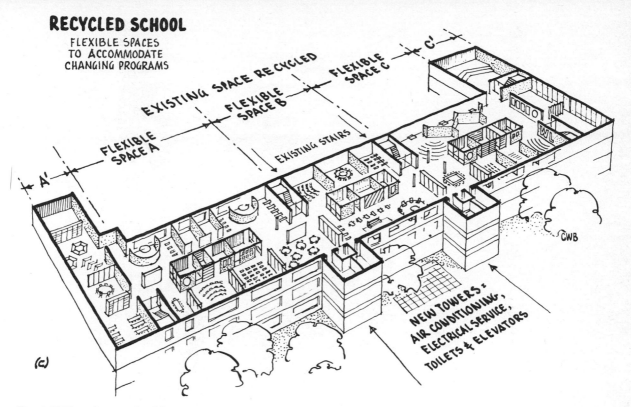

RECYCLED SCHOOL
FLEXIBLE SPACES
TO ACCOMMODATE
CHANGING PROGRAMS

Fig. 4-28 Recycling a school from an existing plan: (a) a typical central corridor school, (b) fixed structural elements, and (c) a new, flexible plan.

who will give credibility to the work of the committee. Viewing and talking and discussing ways to meet objectives should continue for some time, long enough so that all the participants feel that they have really participated but not so long that frustration sets in.

The committee should keep in mind that it is not necessary to commit all the space to specific tasks or departments. Flexible, uncommitted space is valuable in giving the school curriculum a chance to grow in response to changing student needs and a changing student population.

See also Figs. 4-23, 4-24, 4-25, 4-26, and 4-27.

RECYCLED SPACE

The open plan can be developed or recycled from conventional classrooms, especially in schools with a declin-

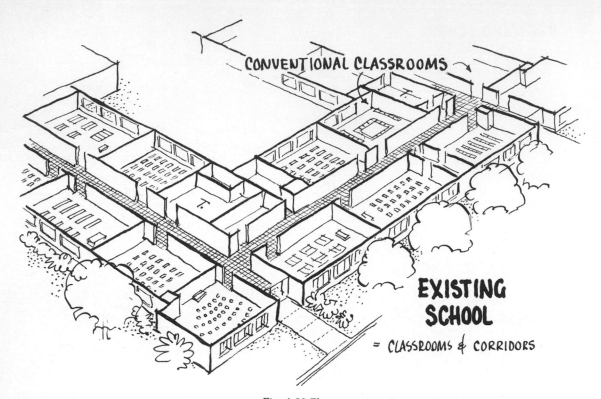

CONVENTIONAL CLASSROOMS

EXISTING SCHOOL

= CLASSROOMS & CORRIDORS

Fig. 4-29 The conventional group of classrooms (above) could be reshaped so that the space is much more varied and flexible (opposite page).

ing student population. A staff architect or a consultant usually can determine which non-load-bearing interior walls can be removed or shifted. Combinations of conventional classrooms can be interspersed with new open-space areas to provide flexibility and openness where it's needed.

Perhaps more important than so-called learning space in a recycled school is the opportunity to create malls and lounges and display areas. These are functional places, but functional places with flavor, openness, and visual quality. They are places where the grace notes of school design can go on view, where the institutional look can be muted or erased.

Everyone concerned about education should fight to keep these places in new schools and work to secure them in remodeled schools. They don't show up by accident or through neglect.

See also Figs. 4-28 and 4-29.

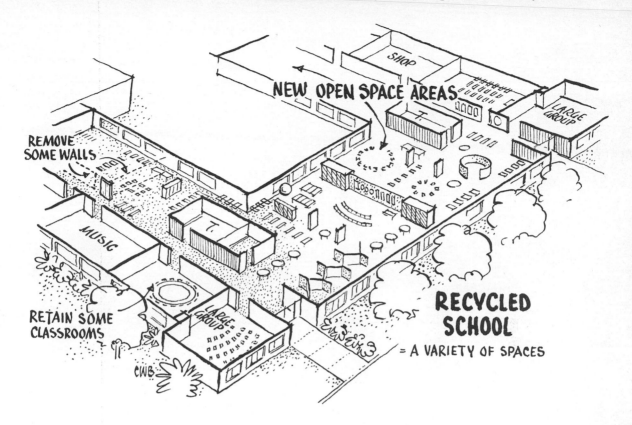

CHAPTER 5

FURNISHING THE ELEMENTARY SCHOOL

■ ■ THE NEXT GENERATION of elementary schools must attempt to link spaces graciously, vary in ceiling height or floor depth, relate to the outdoors effortlessly, and resemble a real landscape—varied, inviting, beckoning one to enter. It will allow groups to come together. It will provide enclosure for variety and fun. It will have style instead of monotony. That is the kind of charge school districts ought to make to architects.

The large, low-ceilinged areas that are characteristic of most open spaces currently in use are not entirely bad. They are modifiable and effective in terms of redeployment of teachers and materials, but they are an outrage in terms of humane environmental qualities. They tell pupils that they are one among many when they should tell pupils that they are special.

Elementary schools should depend on a modifiable environment. The essence of such an environment is that it permits movement on wheels or skids or air cushion systems or similar approaches to seem natural. When furniture can be moved, the environment can be changed. See Figs 5-1 and 5-2.

FURNISHINGS AND MODIFIABLE ENVIRONMENTS IN THE FLEXIBLE ELEMENTARY SCHOOL

The flexible plan can readily be modified. Since everything is furniture and demountable partitions, the only problems are the weight of the equipment when filled and places to move the equipment.

TOP: WEST HILLS ELEMENTARY SCHOOL, NEAR KITTANNING, PA.
BOTTOM: FOREST SCHOOL, NORTH OLMSTED, OHIO.

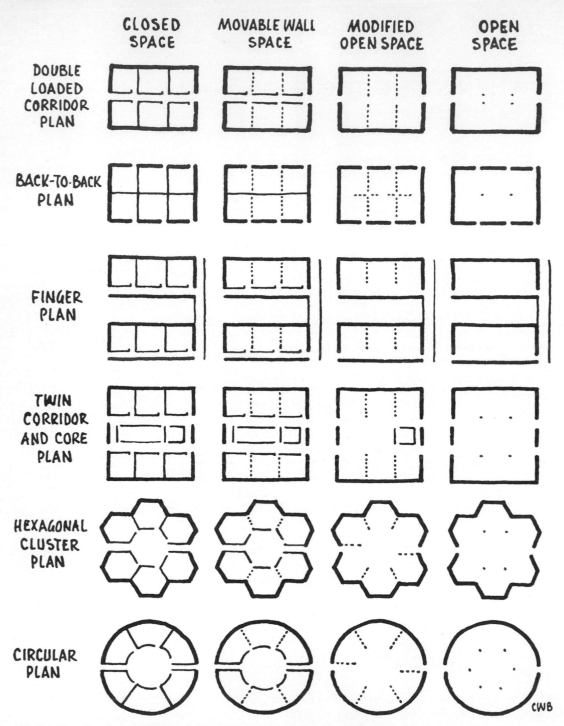

Fig. 5-1 Virtually all school plans can be opened up to produce a modifiable environment that can meet the needs of students and faculty.

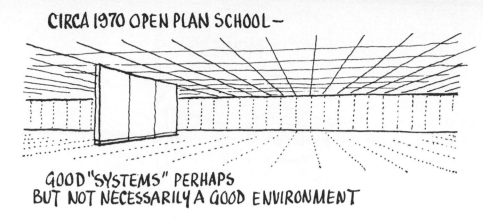

CIRCA 1970 OPEN PLAN SCHOOL—

GOOD "SYSTEMS" PERHAPS
BUT NOT NECESSARILY A GOOD ENVIRONMENT

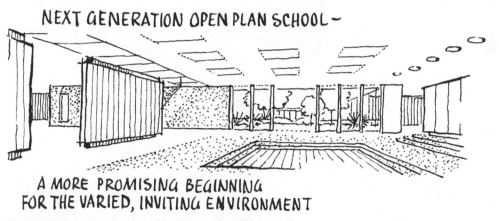

NEXT GENERATION OPEN PLAN SCHOOL—

A MORE PROMISING BEGINNING
FOR THE VARIED, INVITING ENVIRONMENT

Fig. 5-2 The next generation of flexible space will have style instead of monotony and will link spaces graciously.

One of the best ways to study this kind of problem is to use a model, including to scale a green-cloth—covered floor area and templates or scale models of the equipment you are considering. After a staff has exhausted itself in rearranging the furniture, it will have a far better notion of the problems it faces than if it had confined itself to talking. See Figs. 5-3, 5-4, and 5-5.

Table 5-1 lists and describes some of the furnishings that should be considered.

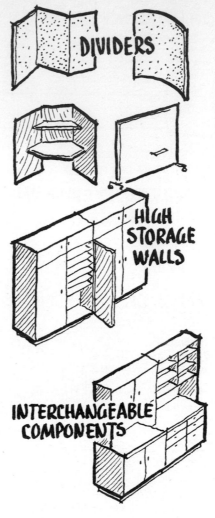

Fig. 5-3 Furnishings such as these
perform a double duty
by breaking up space.

DIVIDERS

HIGH STORAGE WALLS

INTERCHANGEABLE COMPONENTS

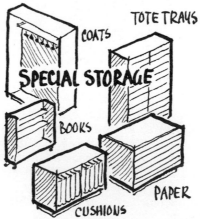

SPECIAL STORAGE

COATS

TOTE TRAYS

BOOKS

CUSHIONS

PAPER

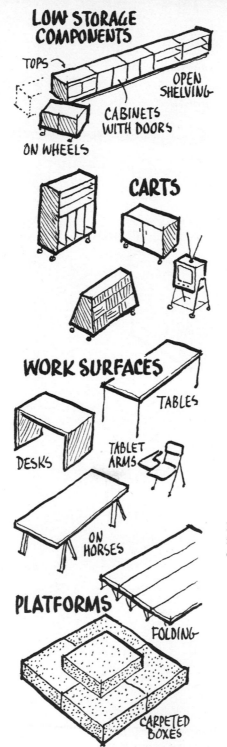

LOW STORAGE COMPONENTS

TOPS

OPEN SHELVING

CABINETS WITH DOORS

ON WHEELS

CARTS

WORK SURFACES

TABLES

DESKS

TABLET ARMS

ON HORSES

PLATFORMS

FOLDING

CARPETED BOXES

Fig. 5-4 All this furniture has one thing in common: it can be moved around quickly with a minimum of fuss.

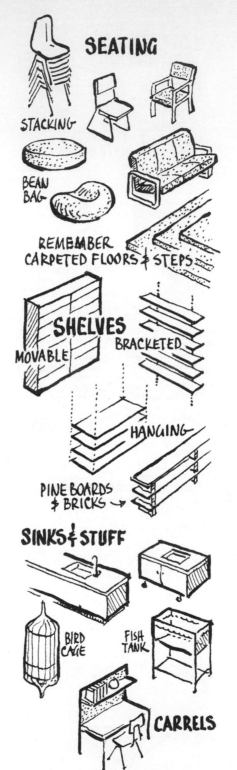

Fig. 5-5 Scale models or templates of
furnishings and equipment can be
used by the staff before purchases are made
so that it can study the available
configurations.

TABLE 5-1 FURNISHINGS IN THE FLEXIBLE PLAN

Kind	Variations	Notes

Dividers	Simple demountable partitions
	Self-supporting
	  Hinged; angled; curved; surfaces used
	  for tack board or chalkboard
		The first thing staffs instinctively look for.
		If an open space is separated by dividers into classroom-like spaces, there is a clear and present message that something isn't working.

	Complex Self-supporting Capable of accepting components: shelves, desk tops, chalk and cork, drawings, tables, etc.	Simple dividers can be used with desks, tables, shelving, etc. Multiuse things cut down on clutter.
	Portable chalkboards and cork boards, some rolling with standards	
High storage components	Self-supporting storage walls	

Interchangeable components	Doors and shelves
	  Locking
	  Nonlocking
		Backs can have cork; most good open plans push these against walls.

	Drawers Combination cabinet and drawers	
High storage components	Coat storage Hanging space in a big box, sometimes wheeled	Back can be chalkboard or cork board.

	Special storage boxes for:
	  Chairs
	  Tables
	  Art supplies
	  Easels
	  Cushions
	  Paper
	  Tote trays
	  Self-learning systems
	  Audio-visual equipment
	  General storage
	  Tool storage
	  Costume storage
	  Music storage
	  Display
		Multiuse.
		Sturdy but light.
		Use back for chalkboard or cork board.
		
		Movable, with large wheels that will move a weight readily over carpet, or portable by use of a simple air cushion, or hung on tracks from the ceiling.

Low storage components	Interchangeable parts
	Counter tops
	Wheeled or otherwise portable
	
	  Cabinets with locks and shelving
	  Cabinets with tote trays	

	Counter tops Drawers: varied sizes	Drawers used for large paper are very heavy units.
	Counter top Open shelving	

(continued)

TABLE 5-1 FURNISHINGS IN THE FLEXIBLE PLAN (Continued)

Kind	Variations	Notes
Carts	Portable over carpet Interchangeable	Carts and low wheeled cabinets are among most useful items in the flexible space
	Audio-visual materials Tool carts Science carts Television cart (high) Book carts (library) Special collections	

Work surfaces	Combined with storage
	Movable
	   Desks
	   Tables
	   Workbench
	   Work counter
	   Tablet or desk armchair
		
		Electric outlets needed.
		Electric outlets needed.

Platforms	Light; portable; nonslip Folding platforms	Relate to ceiling height.
Seating	Chairs Carpeted floor Platform Comfortable furniture: Sofa, etc. Beanbags Inflated furniture	Tend to have too many seats in a large space.
Shelves	Bookshelves	Variable height.
	Open shelving	Basic material organization. Locate where centers of interest or subject matter are located.
Sinks	Provide, using quick connections	Provide safety overflow for waste line when using a quick-connect system.
Wildlife	Environmental chambers Cages Growth chambers Germinating beds	A small sample.
Carrels	Provided as work station, sometimes with electric outlets, sometimes with audio-visual outlets up to complete retrieval system	Use with caution. There is some tendency to overprovide and overequip.

MATERIALS

In the flexible environment, there is a real sense of frustration in the management of materials. These had once been stored in a classroom, handed out to a class, and retrieved. That was simple. If the things that the program anticipates happen, a different way of organizing materials is required.

There are several basic problems. One is that many people—both teachers and children—will use the same materials. A second fact is that an individualized program

TABLE 5-2 MATERIALS AND FLEXIBLE SPACE

Type of material	Examples	Notes on material management
Printed	Reading systems	A variety is made available and organized around a center of interest, perhaps a reading center.
	Mathematics systems	Mathematics center: Materials should be clearly displayed to make sure that they are complete and that children can find them.
	Subject areas Books, pamphlets, charts, maps, etc.	Organized by interest or subject areas: ecology would be interdisciplinary. Science would be organized by subject.
	Games	The increase in interest not only in the mathematics use of games such as Monopoly with young children but in the use of sophisticated simulations means that provision must be made for games, usually in storage cabinets.
Audio-visual	Audio-visual learning systems	Located with a subject or interest center. Electric outlets are important. Storage for components is needed.
	16-millimeter film 8-millimeter film	Brought to teaching area on demand. Use in large group involves acoustic problems; perhaps have a curtain on a track in open space to enclose the area and focus attention. Use a portable screen. It is possible to use rear screen projection with earphones in package units.
	TV tape-recorded materials	Playback provision; three TV monitors and earphones. It is possible to provide permanent TV monitor locations and a wired system, all the way to retrieval.
	Cassettes	Highly portable. Provide storage for cassettes and players; locate as part of interest center.
	Slides, filmstrip, etc.	Locate at interest center. Projectors and electric service are needed.
	Overhead transparencies	Locate at interest center. Projector, tilted screen, and electric outlet are needed.
	Records and tape	Locate at interest center. Provide electric outlets, record or tape players, and earphones.
Supplies	Art Science supplies Workbench Music Paper Audio-visual supplies Blocks Model-making materials	Flexible space works best when there is a logistics center that backs up the flexible area with supplies. Supply cabinets should be located near the point of use.

generates a vast number of individual uses of materials as contrasted with class usage. A third point is that since many of the programs are individualized, there is a quantum leap in the amount and variety of materials. The materials must be organized so that children can find them and the pieces are all present; there is nothing more frustrating than having a study booklet and no response sheet. See also Table 5-2.

TABLE 5-3 HOW TO PUT THE MODIFIABLE ENVIRONMENT TOGETHER

Function	Need	Notes
Teachers are subject specialists.	Material center for each subject.	Children move in groups or individually from one center to another.
Teachers are specialized by approach.	Drillmaster needs materials.	Use of individualized learning systems alternates with presentation and discussion groups. Concentrate materials.
	Large-group presenter needs open space for 100 or some other number of students.	Prepare open space carefully for this grouping. Sound problems are real. Consider a curtain on a ceiling track for enclosure. Heavy use of audio-visual material.
	Teachers are organizers of small discussion and exploration groups.	Disperse comfortable seats, platforms, conversation pits, etc., about the space.
Teachers use individualized instruction intensively.	Interest centers with appropriate materials.	Faculty members move around individual study areas, helping students who need aid. Many students teach other students. A two-student carrel is very useful.
Some group discussion, field work, etc.	Provide for interspersed group spaces.	Strong feeling of available materials of all kinds organized by centers of interest.
Organize by user.	Faculty planning	A collection of tables, storage, and faculty carrel in open space or in closed space off open space.
	Logistics	Central storage; isolated for security. Aides prepare carts and audio-visual equipment and replenish materials.
	Materials	Perhaps centralized in resources center in open space. Staffed by librarian and aides.
	Individualized instruction	Near materials, perhaps centralized in resource area.
	Group work	Varies in size. Locate between individualized instruction and experimentation.
	Experimentation	Active work in science, industrial arts, art.
	Special education	Use all resources. Children requiring special help receive help from staff in small groups. Concentration problems of some children may suggest sound-isolated spaces for such instruction.
	Music	Sound isolation.

FORMING THE MODIFIABLE ENVIRONMENT

The following are generalized approaches that apply to elementary and middle school and nonspecialized high school spaces. Decisions are required as to the way the space will be arranged on the first day. Remember that it is not difficult to change things if you are not happy with the results.

Fig. 5-6 When space is modifiable, students have equal access to all resources; they move around while materials and teachers stay put. Decisions on how space will be organized shape the character of a school's curriculum.

Do not overfurnish. It is far better to underfurnish and add things you need later. One good system is to provide a budget for equipment and furnishings and spend about one-third for the initial installation. Add those things you find you need gradually over the first two or three years of experience with the space.

Decide on the way the space will be organized. If the organization resembles a class of twenty-five children and a teacher, perhaps you should not be building or preparing an open space. A partial list of kinds of organization and their implications is given in Table 5-3. See also Fig. 5-6.

Use models to develop approaches to organization and to experiment with approaches. Put a cadre to work in an extemporized space to try out instructional strategies. Collect or develop materials. The faculty should define roles and role expectations clearly as a preliminary to moving into new space. Roles should be defined basically by organization. Provide for large amounts of time for faculty planning. Move in, and start making changes.

ENCLOSED PLANS AND THE MODIFIABLE ENVIRONMENT

Perhaps the best way to measure the effectiveness of a facility is by seeking the answer to a deceptively simple question: Does the facility provide an appropriate environment for the task to be housed?

The "enclosed plan," to use a generic term, is one that isolates spaces for use through some degree of floor-to-ceiling partitioning. Partitions can be fixed, demountable, or movable as shown in Figs. 5-7 and 5-8 and Table 5-4.

Since the space characteristics of open and enclosed plans can be the same, plans can be changed from open to enclosed to open space upon demand.

Space Characteristics When Demountable Partitions Are Used

Ceiling

There is a modular system related to the wall panels. The ceiling lighting, lighting controls, and, if warm or cool air is introduced by the ceiling, some orderly way to provide the airflow or any ceiling utilities must be designed so that the orderly introduction of walls does not interfere with these functions.

Floor

The floor system is continuous under the partitioning system. If carpet or resilient tile is used, the material

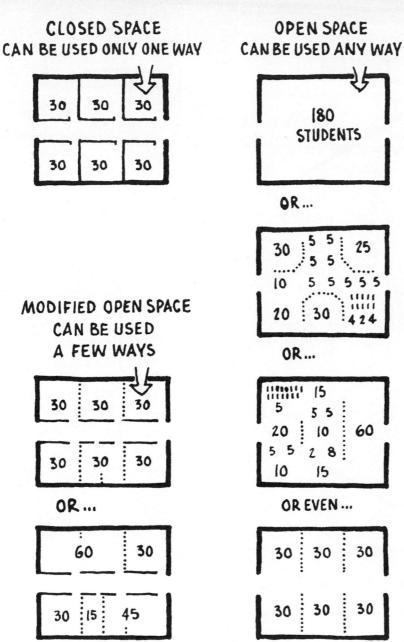

CLOSED SPACE
CAN BE USED ONLY ONE WAY

| 30 | 30 | 30 |
| 30 | 30 | 30 |

OPEN SPACE
CAN BE USED ANY WAY

180 STUDENTS

OR...

30	5 5	25
	5 5	
10	5 5 5 5 5	
20	30	4 2 4

OR...

	15	
5	5 5	
20	10	60
5 5	2 8	
10	15	

MODIFIED OPEN SPACE
CAN BE USED
A FEW WAYS

| 30 | 30 | 30 |
| 30 | 30 | 30 |

OR...

| 60 | 30 |
| 30 | 15 | 45 |

OR EVEN...

| 30 | 30 | 30 |
| 30 | 30 | 30 |

Fig 5-7 Partitions can be used to modify space in many ways, including a design that follows the traditional thirty-student classroom organization.

extends under the partitions so that it is simple to change the partition location. Any existing floor services must be responsive to the grid in which the partition system works.

AN ENCLOSED SPACE ...
TEACHING AUDITORIUM...

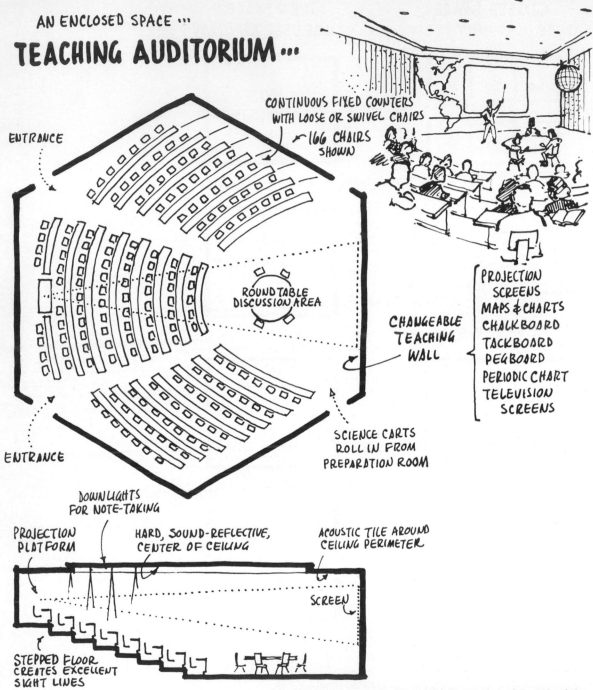

ENTRANCE

CONTINUOUS FIXED COUNTERS
WITH LOOSE OR SWIVEL CHAIRS
166 CHAIRS SHOWN

ROUND TABLE
DISCUSSION AREA

CHANGEABLE
TEACHING
WALL

PROJECTION
SCREENS
MAPS & CHARTS
CHALKBOARD
TACKBOARD
PEGBOARD
PERIODIC CHART
TELEVISION
SCREENS

ENTRANCE

SCIENCE CARTS
ROLL IN FROM
PREPARATION ROOM

DOWNLIGHTS
FOR NOTE-TAKING

PROJECTION
PLATFORM

HARD, SOUND-REFLECTIVE,
CENTER OF CEILING

ACOUSTIC TILE AROUND
CEILING PERIMETER

SCREEN

STEPPED FLOOR
CREATES EXCELLENT
SIGHT LINES

Fig. 5-8 Instead of being unused for large parts of the school day, most school auditoriums can be transformed into teaching space for demonstrations and audio-visual presentations.

TABLE 5-4   REPRESENTATIVE PARTITIONING SYSTEMS FOR ENCLOSED SPACE

Kind	Varieties	Notes
Fixed (relatively)	Bearing partitions Partitions heavily related to utilities	Although both types of partitions can be moved, these are frequently costly and time-consuming tasks. In new construction, avoid these or locate them where the main space can be changed.
Demountable	Non-wall-bearing masonry such as concrete block	Inexpensive; relatively simple to change. However, the process is dirty and takes time.

	Panel system
	(many types available)
		Systems vary in cost. Where labor costs are high, these systems may be as inexpensive as painted concrete block.
		
		Desirable characteristics to look for when making selection:
		    Good sound reduction.
		    Durability.
		    Good-quality finishes.
		    Locks to ceiling system.
		    Electric wiring integral or easy to install.
		    Accepts panel for light controls, heat and cooling controls, clock, audio-visual and retrieval system.
		    Attractiveness.
		    Guaranteed easy and inexpensive to move.
		Low initial cost.

Movable	Folding partition (many kinds available)	Expensive; allows for space to be open or closed on demand with little energy required in the change.
		
		Desirable characteristics to look for when making selection:
		    Good sound reduction when closed.
		    Durability.
		    Attractiveness.
		    Good-quality finishes.
		    Wall is usable when closed.
		    Ease in operation.
		    Good hardware.

Psychology of Walls

Walls generally look fixed. Even when they are demountable, most users expect them to be there tomorrow. Here are some theories on walls in schools that you might want to test:

1. Omit some walls that you may want, and have them installed when the faculty is there. First put them in the wrong place, and then erect them in the correct place and try to show the doubters how simple the process is.

2. When deciding upon walls, leave them out when in

doubt. It is easier to add walls later if you find you need them. You can even buy panels beyond your minimum needs for use as security blankets.

3. Be careful when a demand is made for movable walls. Translated, this means: "I am modern and up to date. I want flexibility. I have no intention of using it." There is an inertial quality about these walls. With a few exceptions, the walls when closed tend to remain closed and when opened tend to remain open. Movable walls are expensive ways to avoid change.

4. One of the real bonuses that comes with reduction in partitioning is the increase in usable space. When a series of small rooms is provided, a surprising amount of corridor is involved. The more open the plan, the more travel routes that do not take up the space required by a corridor network.

5. It is not necessary to name a room after every function in the school. Designate an area instead if you want to memorialize an idea.

Floor-to-Ceiling Partitions as Furniture

The demountable partition can be far more than a mere room divider. It can become part of a system for hanging equipment and furniture in the room. A fully detailed partition system could accept chalkboard and tack board, receive supports for shelving, and serve to hang a desk or similar accessories to the wall.

Use of Demountable Partitions in Educational Settings

A variety of subsystems is involved in the selection of an environment responsive to change. Among them are the following.

1. Humility: Members of a traditional classroom-oriented faculty may say that they want separate, distinct classrooms, but they are willing to admit that the teachers who succeed them may not. Accordingly, if the cost premium is not too high, install demountable partitions since change could occur.

2. Transition: A faculty, happy and experienced in the use of classrooms, sees limited uses for open space and tries it out. One small move follows another.

3. Systematic choice: A faculty confident of its abilities defines the activity of a group of children sufficiently well to make good decisions about what works best for the children in open and in enclosed space. This faculty is using the technology of space effectively.

4. Variety: There is nothing so dull as one idea,

whether of openness or enclosure, that is followed slavishly. The idea of a secret garden or a surprise around the corner is still valid for both adults and children.

5. Time: It is surprising that schools do not consciously consider time as a function of a change in setting. This is a response to a child or a group of children who may move from the small group of early childhood to the larger group of the middle years of schooling. It is possible to start a year in classrooms and regularly reduce the number of walls, putting two groups together when the children will profit from the experience and increasing the sense of openness during the year. If a program so requires, it should be possible to replace walls in an open space as the seasons change. Toward the end of the year, twelve seminar rooms may be required to assemble ideas and to serve as the home base and work space for a team of students; over a weekend install them in open space.

WHEELS FOR MODIFIABLE ENVIRONMENTS

In a modifiable environment wheels mean the delivery system for materials. (Instead of wheels, an air cushion or track or vacuum tube or electronics may be used.) Examples of such delivery systems would include:

- A cart wheeled down a corridor to bring a TV monitor to a classroom.
- A science cart bringing electronic instrumentation to a wet (test-tube) laboratory.
- A library cart. Books need not be in fixed stacks. Perhaps the whole library should move out to the users.
- Art on a cart.
- A cart full of individualized learning packets in mathematics, taken back to be replenished and brought out when needed.
- Food on a cart.
- A rapid print-out machine connected to a computer at the publishers, delivering materials in printed book form electronically.
- A TV tape recorder recording a program from a central source ten states away.
- Skill sequences for industrial arts (packets) brought out for use and returned to storage.
- A computer-controlled delivery system in which an unmanned vehicle brings materials to the point of use.
- A vacuum-tube system that delivers material rapidly.
- An audio-visual retrieval system that produces sound and pictures where needed and when needed.

It is clear that as a school becomes more individualized and less of a group, more miniaturized and less full-scale, better accustomed to use the community and less reliant on creating replicas in the school, the school building will be less specialized and more interdisciplinary. In consequence, a delivery system is of great importance.

Schools have lots of labor. Students may be the best delivery system until the quantity of material becomes so staggering that the human labor required to move it takes too much time away from the process of using the material. At that point, sophisticated delivery systems will be required.

PLANNING FURNITURE AND EQUIPMENT FOR FLEXIBLE SPACE AT THE LOWER PRIMARY (KINDERGARTEN–SECOND GRADE) LEVEL

As we have suggested, in an elementary school the variety of group sizes, the variety of work, and the elastic use of space demand constant rearrangement of furniture and different combinations of items. Furniture can be the most important way in which teachers achieve flexibility. See Fig. 5-9.

A flexible plan with an uninviting appearance will induce more sleep than interest among teachers and pupils. Equipment plays a large part in the overall effectiveness of open planning. Keep three simple criteria in mind. The space should (1) be a place that a child can dominate rather than be dominated by; (2) encourage movement of pupils, allowing the immediate formation of groups of any size to suit educational needs; and (3) provide comfort, beauty, and stimulation.

In addition to the usual criteria of durability, safety, and pleasing design, all major categories of furniture and equipment (seating, work surfaces, storage, display, play, and so forth) should meet the following requirements:

1. Easy mobility: Many so-called mobile items on the market today are so heavy or so poorly balanced that the average teacher simply cannot move them without substantial assistance. It should not be necessary to request janitorial aid and wait until such aid becomes available in order to rearrange mobile equipment or furniture. To achieve a truly flexible, creative atmosphere, the equipment and furniture must be easily moved.

2. Multipurpose use: Double-duty products can conserve space and money. Minimizing quantity is very important in the flexible-plan concept since so much is on view in a given space. Also, just as it is desirable to have many kinds of things on view to stimulate the student's

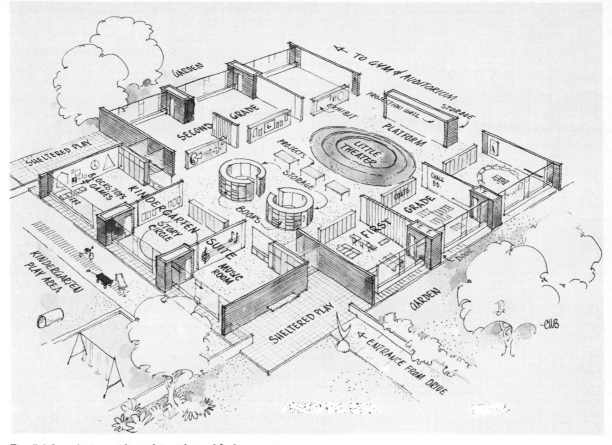

Fig. 5-9 In a design such as this with modified open space, rearrangement of the furniture and walls can move the flow of the program toward or away from traditional patterns to conform to any approach the staff decides to follow.

imagination and lead to an exciting atmosphere of virtually unlimited educational resources, it is equally desirable to limit quantities of the same things.

3. Harmony: Seek a range of related items of equipment and furniture that can be selected in any combination and deployed in a multitude of different ways and yet avoid visual chaos, or the inhibition created by items of unrelated dimensions. To achieve this goal, every item must share three attributes: related dimensional system, related color specification, and related materials specification.

4. Aesthetic achievement: Pleasing design concepts, which make the item good to look at as well as functional, are essential if a ho-hum effect is to be erased.

There are several areas in which you can expect to encounter specific problems:

1. Seating: The solution to the seating problem need not be universally applicable. Children would presumably prefer a choice; carpeted floor, cushions, lounge chairs or sofas, and platforms with a carpeted surface all can serve in association with conventional seating and homey touches, such as a few rocking chairs or items such as inflatable plastic or beanbag-type chairs or cushions.

2. Work surfaces: Work surfaces should be easily moved and modular. If these items are on wheels, the wheels should be lockable. Some thought should be given to coordination with seating design. Items should be available in a wide variety of heights (standing, lying on floor) and shapes. Standing heights could accommodate storage below. It should be possible to group these items to create large work surfaces. Consideration should be given to easy availability of electricity at the working surfaces, both for the use of audio-visual devices as in an audio-tutorial situation and to supplement overhead lighting.

3. Storage and display: A number of good items on the general market meet most of the design criteria we have outlined. Clothing storage can present a problem. Even though available storage units may be quite handsome and easily portable, by the time twenty or thirty coats with attendant dripping galoshes and umbrellas have been piled onto them the vision presented does not meet a high aesthetic standard. Clothing storage may be one item that might best be part of the permanent fixtures.

A list of equipment for an instructional area to accommodate 200 children is presented in Table 5-5.

Notes on Equipment

The funds set aside for equipment should be budgeted over the first year or so of operation. The suggested quantities in Table 5-6 should be regarded as minimal. The staff would evaluate these items in terms of quantities, quality, and function during the year. Additions or changes would be made in terms of what the staff needs to implement the program as it develops.

Seating should be selected from a combination of conventional stacking chairs, cushions, carpeted floors, platforms, steps, benches, stools, lounge furniture, beanbag chairs, puncture-proof inflatable chairs, rocking chairs, a sawhorse, a tabletop, a ladder, a multiuse cube, a large rubber ball, or even a telephone book. It may not be

TABLE 5-5   PRIMARY INSTRUCTIONAL AREA FOR 200 CHILDREN

Equipment	Suggested quantity
A-frame sawhorse brace with connector bar, 4 inches wide by 40 inches long, with a height of 12 inches, for use as a base for resting ladders and panels, as a balance beam, and as something to climb	6
Ladder, 48 inches long by 12 inches wide, with round rungs 10 inches apart	3
Stair-platform unit, approximately 16 inches high, with two 8-inch steps at the sides; 36 inches square at the top	3
Square portable platform, 4 feet by 4 feet by 16 inches high, for use also as a low writing surface; caster base. If a removable top is supplied, this unit could serve for storage	8
Mobile storage cabinet, approximately 24 by 48 inches by 30 inches high, with 20 removable tote trays, 11 by 20 inches by 4 inches deep; doors and back with tack board finish; caster base; rack for smock storage	10
Mobile wardrobe rack, 24 by 48 inches by 60 inches high; double-face unit with 25-coat capacity, with provision for 2-student compartments on each side; caster base. An alternative would be built-in coat-hat-boot racks, thus eliminating this item.	8
Mobile open shelving, 24 by 48 inches by 36 inches high; adjustable shelves; caster base	10
Mobile flat paper storage cabinet with six 4-inch drawers, 28 by 48 inches by 30 inches high; caster base	8
Wooden rocking chair, with a seat approximately 12 inches high	10
Lightweight easy-glide seating with seat heights of approximately 11 and 13 inches; stacking feature desirable. These could be stools, stacking chairs, or multipurpose units such as simple cubes.	85
Plastic-top round table, 48 inches in diameter; adjustable height	8
Plastic-top round folding table, 48 inches in diameter and 20 inches in height; 3-inch casters	4
Plastic-surface trapezoid tables, 30 by 30 by 30 by 60 inches; adjustable height; capable of accepting tote trays on tray support runners	48
Rectangular table, 48 by 30 inches by 30-inch maximum adjustable height, for possible use as teacher station and for use as standing-height work station	16
A-frame double-face mobile bookcase with a display rack; 40 by 48 inches by 36 inches high; caster base	8
High-base seating, with adjustable seat height of 27 to 32 inches and swivel seat with adjustable posture back, or standard teacher's chair	8
Edge-grain maple craft or art bench suitable for hammering, 60 by 42 inches by 24 inches high, with casters, vise, and storage below	4
Folding painting easels; adjustable height	16
Mobile panel space divider on casters, approximately 48 inches wide by 54 inches high, engineered to be freestanding or to be joined to other panels; capable of having chalkboard, tack board, or mirror surface attached and of accepting equipment (adjustable shelving, work surface, file unit, etc.) on surface	16
Mobile animal cage, 36 by 20 inches by 24 inches high	2
Mobile planter, 36 by 18 inches by 18 inches high	4
Privacy booth or listening carrel; possibly a totally enclosed unit with a reasonable crawl-through entrance; possibly wired for sound (music, storytelling)	4
Mobile costume rack (hanger rack reachable by small children), preferably adjustable, approximately 50 inches wide by 18 inches deep, by 48 inches high, providing closed storage for hats, feathers, and shoes. The back could be provided with a full-length mirror.	2
Mobile bin, 24 inches wide by 20 inches long by 22 inches deep	8
Mobile musical instrument rack for rhythm instruments, possibly containing a record or tape player	3
Floor cushions. Consider several varieties and shapes.	18
Lounge chairs with stain-resistant upholstery	6
Mobile storage cases, approximately 68 inches in height, with a modular capacity to accept a variety of drawer sizes, adjustable shelves, or special-purpose trays. A double-door unit 47 inches wide by 23 inches deep by 68 inches high might be equipped, as one example of a choice of interiors, with 2 full-width shelves placed 30 inches apart, 4 half-width drawers 6 inches high, and 4 half-width drawers 9 inches high.	8

necessary to provide conventional chair-desk arrangements for every child.

Although most of the floor area would be carpeted, some portion might be hard-surfaced for the indoor use of wheeled toys, water play, art and craft work, or dance activities. Consider a removable waterproof floor covering.

Electric outlets should be readily available for the use of audio-visual equipment. Light control is less of a problem today because of the introduction of projection screens usable in full daylight, although attention still must be paid to this factor. Audio-visual equipment should be portable and be provided with storage-transport carts for use throughout the space.

Available on the market are several equipment systems employing mobile working walls that accommodate many coordinated components: chalkboards, display panels, storage cabinets, work surfaces, and specialized storage racks. Should such a system be contemplated, the number of mobile storage cabinets or simple panel space dividers would be reduced accordingly.

PLANNING FURNITURE AND EQUIPMENT FOR FLEXIBLE SPACE AT THE UPPER PRIMARY (THIRD-SIXTH GRADE) LEVEL

Space for this upper elementary unit would accommodate two groups of 200 students, or a total of 400 students, with 40 square feet per student. The total space would thus be 16,000 square feet.

The space can be subdivided in function to serve as centers for study in communication arts, science, mathematics, and social studies. Since about the same amount of time will be required in each area of study, approximately 4,000 square feet of space may be used for each center for study. In general, the centers for study should surround the instructional materials center. Sound-isolated spaces, measuring 300 square feet each, should be provided within the allotment, with one for each of the four subject areas. Faculty planning should be located within the open space used for each center for study.

Although most of the floor area would be carpeted, some portion should be hard-surfaced and chemically resistant for use by science, art, and communication arts. Other activities also will best take place on a hard surface.

The equipment criteria suggested for the ungraded primary unit will also apply here. In the following suggested equipment list, note the differences in height of many items.

- Bright-colored cushions with tough plastic covers, approximately 24 by 18 inches by 4 inches thick
- Overstuffed chair with a washable cover
- 2-student trapezoid tables, approximately 48 by 24 inches by an adjustable height of 22 to 29 inches

- Stool with a backrest; adjustable height of 16 to 22 inches
- Plastic-surface standing-height work tables, 30 inches deep by 60 inches long by 27 to 29 inches high; capable of being grouped end to end to form work counters
- Open-top mobile bin, 24 by 10 inches 22 inches high
- Aquarium-terrarium with a mobile stand
- Square portable platform, 4 by 4 feet by 8 inches high
- Rectangular portable platform, 4 by 8 feet with an elevation of 16 inches; with folding legs or hollow for storage
- Trapezoidal platform, 36 by 18 by 24 inches by 8 inches high
- Rectangular portable platform, 4 by 8 feet by 24 inches in elevation
- Mobile storage cabinet with removable tote trays, approximately 14 by 20 inches by 4 inches deep, with a rack for smock storage; doors and back with a tack board finish
- Mobile wardrobe rack, 68 by 22 inches by 50 inches high, with adjustable rack height; shoe compartments and hat shelf; possibly a fixed item
- Mobile open shelving on wheels, 52 inches long by 24 inches wide by 43 inches high, with 4 shelves or cutouts to accommodate tote trays
- Mobile flat paper storage cabinet, 24 by 47 inches by 40 inches high
- Lightweight easy-glide seating with a seat height of approximately 12 to 15 inches, available in bright colors; stacking feature
- Plastic-top round table, 48 inches in diameter; adjustable height
- Plastic-top folding round table on wheels, 48 inches in diameter and 22 inches high
- Rectangular table, 48 by 30 inches, with a maximum adjustable height of 29 inches
- A-frame double-face mobile bookcase and display rack; 48 inches wide by 36 inches high
- High-base seating with adjustable seat height of 27 to 32 inches and swivel seat with adjustable posture back, or standard teacher's chair
- 3-panel space divider on casters, with chalkboard and tack board covering (chalkboard should nearly reach the floor)
- Mobile panel, 48 inches wide by 54 inches high, with a mirror on one side and a tack board on other
- Freestanding curved partition, 60 inches wide by 54 inches high, with a surface suitable for attaching drawing paper to create panoramas and cycloramas

- Testing carrel with a work surface height of 24 inches (auxiliary lighting possibly necessary)
- Easily moved piano; spinet or electronic with amplifier and plug-in earphone options; also stool of adjustable height
- Demountable partitions as needed

SPECIALIZED CENTERS FOR STUDY

Science

- Acid-resistant demonstration desk, 42 inches high by 36 inches wide by 60 inches long, equipped with several drawers; cupboard for the storage of ordinary equipment; open space for a tote box of temporary storage; 2 two-way gas cocks; 2 double 110-volt alternating-current outlets; water; chemical-resistant large sink with trap
- Laboratory truck, 42 inches high by 36 inches wide by 36 inches long, with rubber-covered wheels and an acid-resistant top surface, equipped with a metal-lined tray at the bottom and adjustable open shelves above tray (wheels with braking device)
- Sink counter, 34 inches high by 22 inches deep by 96 inches long, with a double-door base cabinet with adjustable shelves and two 4-drawer base units, each 18 by 16 inches by 10 inches deep; pegboard drying rack above
- Portable 4-student science table, 36 by 72 inches by 36 inches high, complete with sink and four 2-foot removable aluminum posts; self-contained water service; 110-volt alternating-current receptacles and 6-foot extension cord
- Display case and microscope storage, 36 by 24 inches by 60 inches high with lockable sliding glass doors; approximately 6 adjustable shelves
- 3-drawer legal-size file case
- Mobile germinating bed and table, 60 by 24 by 34 inches
- 2-student science table, 54 by 24 by 29 inches, with chemical-resistant plastic top
- Adjustable stools

Mathematics

The general equipment listed should suffice for the most part in this study center. You might consider additional display cases with sliding glass doors for specialized equipment that should be visible.

Social Studies

The general equipment listed should also suffice for the most part in this center. You might consider specialized mobile map or display racks with locking wheels.

Communication Arts

- Typing or sound-controlled carrel, 46 inches high by 36 inches wide by 26 inches deep; acoustically treated
- Mobile costume rack
- Stair platform unit
- Portable stage unit
- Puppet theater
- Drafting table, 60 by 36 inches; adjustable height
- Mobile drying rack, 48 by 25 inches by 36 inches high, with approximately 15 shelves
- Glass-enclosed soundproof module, 128 by 113 by 95 inches
- 4-drawer file case with lock
- Folding easel with adjustable height
- Display cubes
- Art table approximately 36 by 24 inches by 30 inches high, with pedestal of 3 locked drawers and adjustable top (40 degrees from horizontal plane)

The panel system will provide display surfaces. Presumably audio-visual equipment will be entirely portable and will be provided with storage-transport carts for use throughout the school.

INSTRUCTIONAL MATERIALS CENTER: SPACE NEEDS

	Square feet
Up to 60 students (40 square feet each)	2,400
10,000 pieces of information ($^1/_{10}$ square foot each)	1,000
Support space:	
Librarian's work space	300
Audio-visual storage and work space	200
Graphics area for faculty use	300
TV and audio taping	200
Total	4,400

Circulation Desk System

- Card catalog unit, 13 inches high by 35 inches wide by 18 inches deep, with 15 drawers
- 2-row card tray unit, 4 inches high by 7 inches wide by 16 inches deep
- Mobile book bin, 32 inches high by 32 inches wide by 18 inches deep
- Interior book return unit, 41 inches high by 36 inches wide by 17 inches deep
- Freestanding card catalog unit, 42 inches high by 32 inches wide by 24 inches deep, with 30 drawers
- Study carrels, D/F, 50 inches high overall by 36 inches wide by 48 inches deep; work surface 25 inches high
- Quadrangular study carrel, 50 inches high overall by 70 inches wide by 70 inches deep
- Stand-up reference table, 72 inches wide by 41 inches high by 24 inches deep (12 square feet, or 3 stations)
- Map case, 47 inches high by 45 inches wide by 38 inches deep, with 5 drawers
- Freestanding display case, 40 inches high by 36 inches wide by 36 inches deep, with interior lighting
- Newspaper rack, 29 inches high by 33 inches wide by 31 inches deep
- Book truck, 38 inches high by 30 inches wide by 14 inches deep
- Atlas stand, 40 inches high by 30 inches wide by 28 inches deep
- Dictionary stand, 40 inches high by 30 inches wide by 28 inches deep
- High-base seating with adjustable seat height of 20 to 27 inches and swivel seat with adjustable posture back
- Reading table, approximately 26 inches high by 72 inches wide by 48 inches deep
- Reading table, approximately 26 inches high by 48 inches in diameter
- Lounge seating 3
- Lounge chair
- Magazine table, 24 inches in diameter
- End table, 30 by 18 inches by 15 inches high
- Chair with a seat 16 inches high
- Single-face shelving, mobile if possible
- Double-face shelving, mobile if possible
- Magazine shelving and display
- Tote tray storage cabinet for audio-visual supply packages
- Specialized storage units:
  Film cartridge

Filmstrip
Audio tapes
Flat print storage
Record storage
Tall cabinets with adjustable shelving for tape recorders, projectors, etc.

Librarian's Work Space

- 2-drawer mobile file with locking wheels
- Upholstered posture chair; adjustable seat height and backrest
- Side chair with upholstered seat and back, or stacking type
- Mobile typing stand, 26 inches high, with folding leaves 22 inches wide closed and 51 inches wide extended; wheels with locking device
- Counter with sink, approximately 6 feet long, with storage above and below
- Plastic-top stacking table, 60 by 36 inches by 29 inches high
- Desk, 60 by 36 inches by 29 inches high, with conference overhang; or modular unit used in conjunction with panels accepting desk unit
- Freestanding joinable privacy panels, 80 inches high by 48 inches wide, with tack board surface

Graphics Area

- Editing counter, approximately 6 feet by 24 inches by 30 inches, with wall shelving
- Lockable storage case, 36 by 18 inches by 72 inches high, with 5 shelves
- Storage case, 36 by 18 inches by 72 inches high, with 7 shelves, compartmentalized for tape and film storage
- Plastic-top stacking table, 60 by 36 inches by 29 inches high
- Chair with a seat 16 inches high
- 4-drawer file case with lock
- Folding chair with a seat 17 inches high
- Adjustable drafting table, 60 by 36 by 42 inches
- Transparency maker
- Small offset press or duplicating machine
- Sink

TV and Audio Taping

This area requires a work counter with ample electric outlets and TV reception outlets, chairs, and storage. The entire area should be soundproof and glass-enclosed.

FACULTY AND STAFF SPACE

	Square feet
Faculty lounge	300
Staff toilets and cot space (2 at 150 square feet each)	300
Waiting area	. . .*
Secretarial space	150
Principal's office	150
Conference room	250
Specialist's offices	
Learning disabilities, psychologist, and similar staff (3 at 100 square feet each)	300
Work space	200
Storage	200
Total	1,850

*In Instructional Materials Center.

If faculty and staff units are treated as separate spaces, in cases in which privacy is advisable, the required furnishings are obvious. If some of the areas can be treated as open areas, then the action office approach to furniture and equipment should be considered. The term "action office" refers to modular units that are interchangeable and are attachable to privacy panels used to create semiprivate areas of activity. This solution is, of course, the most versatile.

HEALTH UNIT SPACE

	Square feet
Nurse	150
Waiting area	100
Examining area	150
Cot rooms with toilet (2 at 100 square feet each)	200
Total	600

This area should be located near the younger children. By its nature it must be divided into separate areas and will be furnished and equipped accordingly:

- Side chair with upholstered seat and back
- Lounge or bench seating 3
- A-frame, double-face mobile bookcase and display rack, 48 inches wide by 36 inches high
- Tackboard (as much as possible)
- Single-pedestal desk, 60 by 30 by 29 inches high
- Posture chair; adjustable seat height and backrest
- 4-drawer file case with lock

- Wardrobe and storage case
- Sink counter with storage below
- Examination table
- Scale
- Adjustable examination lamp
- Stool, approximately 15 inches high
- Cart, 24 by 18 inches by 30 inches high, with locking wheels and shelf
- Storage cabinet with lock
- Rest cot with Naugahyde or other waterproof upholstery; clamp for paper cover

SPECIAL INSTRUCTIONAL SPACES

	Square feet
Music room (vocal music), related closely to major instructional areas	800
Art room	
Essentially this room is headquarters for an art teacher who for the most part works in the large flexible areas. This space is storage, has special materials such as clay bins and kilns (with appropriate wiring), and offers opportunities for advanced or concentrated work to some students.	800
Physical education	
The gymnasium is also a special space for community use. Consequently, it is sized for basketball, using a playing court measuring 84 by 50 feet. This will require a room of 100 by 60 feet as a minimum, possibly of 100 by 70 feet.	7,000
Total	8,600

VOCAL MUSIC EQUIPMENT SUGGESTIONS

- Straight posture music chair with folding tablet arm, approximately 16 inches in height
- Conductor's podium chair-stand, with upholstered seat and back, swivel seat, balanced standing platform
- Mobile music folio cabinet, 28 inches wide by 17 inches deep by 36 inches high; 40 folders
- Concert-style desk-top conductor's center, 31 inches

wide, adjustable for height on top of cabinet with storage; wheeled
- Easily moved piano; adjustable stool
- Mobile wardrobe rack, approximately 56 by 20 by 60 inches; 30-garment capacity

Size, shape, and construction material are important factors in planning and designing music facilities for the best sound control possible. The architect should aim for a room that has optimum reverberation time, even distribution of sound, and freedom from undesirable absorption of certain pitches. Nonparallel walls or splayed walls and ceilings should be considered; soundproof walls and doors are desirable. Provide doors 6 feet wide so that a piano can be moved in and out. Other equipment includes a chalkboard with music ruling on part of it, a pull-type screen over chalkboard, and a bulletin board. Also consider provision for music recording and reproduction. Audio-visual equipment should include a record player, a tape recorder, and possibly a television receiver. Provide adequate electric outlets for audio-visual equipment.

ART EQUIPMENT SUGGESTIONS
- Work counter approximately 12 feet long, with 2 deep hot- and cold-water sinks, tool board, and cabinets above and below
- Work counter, approximately 16 feet long, with knee spaces and cupboards below
- Mobile storage cabinet with removable tote trays
- Mobile flat paper storage cabinet
- Wardrobe and storage case, approximately 36 by 18 inches by 82 inches high
- Single-pedestal desk, 60 by 30 inches by 29 inches high
- Posture chair with upholstered seat and back
- Side chair
- 4-drawer file case
- Art table with locked-drawer pedestal and adjustable top
- Stool with backrest, adjustable in height from 16 to 22 inches
- Adjustable drafting table, 60 by 36 by 42 inches
- Mobile open shelving, 52 inches long by 24 inches wide by 43 inches high; on wheels with locking device
- Mobile panel, 48 inches wide by 54 inches high, with a mirror on one side and a tack board on the other
- Maple-top craft bench, 64 by 28 by 36 inches, with a steel leg base and vise attachment

- Enameling kiln with a chamber measuring 8 by 10 by 4 inches
- Folding floor-type loom, with 4 harnesses
- Table-type loom, with 24-inch reed
- Damp cabinet, 48 by 24 by 36 inches
- Open steel drying rack with sides, 36 by 18 by 84 inches
- Ceramics kiln with a chamber measuring 18 by 18 by 18 inches
- Kick potter's wheel, approximately 32 by 25 inches
- Electric potter's wheel, 32 by 25 inches
- Mobile clay cart, 20 by 22 by 18 inches

PHYSICAL EDUCATION EQUIPMENT SUGGESTIONS

- Rectangular swing-up basketball backstop, of wood (glass if budget permits)
- Plain and knotted climbing ropes
- Rope hoist
- Mats, 6 by 12 feet, approximately 2 inches thick; capable of being tied together to form one large mat
- Mat truck
- Balance beam, 4 inches wide by approximately 12 feet long
- Base for support of balance beams and ladder; pyramid shape for stability, 12 by 20 inches by 30 inches high
- Ladder, 8 feet long
- Rocker board, approximately 5 feet long
- Teeterboard with center-pivot base, 8 feet long
- Wall-mounted chinning bars
- Rope, sometimes used with tire attached as a tire swing, or simply knotted as a swing
- Imaginative structure for climbing to develop muscular coordination and balance
- Wheeled cart similar to shopping cart for transporting game equipment
- Volleyball net standards with floor plates

PHYSICAL EDUCATION SPACE NEEDS

If the entire upper primary school of 400 students has physical education twice a week, 800 weekly student-hours of time are involved. If sections of 30 students meet with two instructors, the gym can accommodate in one day, for one hour a section, 360 weekly student-hours (30 students per section times 2 sections per hour times 6 hours). Thus, using the gymnasium half time would accommodate the twice-weekly physical education requirement. Because the lower primary school population of 200 students would also use physical education facilities, the gymnasium facilities would be used nearly full time. Since students now in grades 5 and 6 shower after physical education, adequate locker and shower rooms are required.

Dressing, lockers, and shower areas:

Girls		Square feet
30 girls dressing and dressing lockers	400	
10 showers (25 square feet each)	250	
Toilet	100	
Physical education instructor	100	
Storage	100	
Boys (same space breakdown)	950	1,900
Gymnasium		7,000
Storage off gymnasium floor (2 at 200 square feet)		400
Stage (used also for instrumental music)		1,200
Total		10,500

Fig. 5-10 Traditional physical education facility.

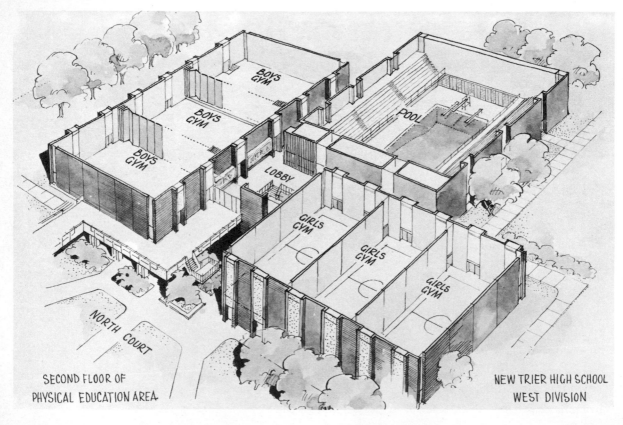

SECOND FLOOR OF
PHYSICAL EDUCATION AREA

NEW TRIER HIGH SCHOOL
WEST DIVISION

Storage must be provided for seating if the area is used as an auditorium. Stacking chairs of varying heights to accommodate children of all ages will most probably be used. Folding mats and seating on floor cushions might be used in lieu of stacking chairs. Consider the need for instrument storage as well.

Gymnasiums, particularly if they are large and the floor surface is tough, can accommodate a wide range of functions. Dances, roller-skating, assemblies, dramatics, banquets, exhibits, and the like are among the activities that, along with basketball, large spectator audiences, badminton, jogging, and calisthenics, can take place in these versatile structures. See Fig. 5-10.

Further increase in the ability of gymnasiums to change space and function is related to two factors. One is the size of the enclosure. The other is the portability of separate items of environment. As the size of the enclosure increases, the variety of possible functions increases. Moreover, it is possible to work around fixed items of equipment or to push them to one side to make room for other functions. The portability of large pieces of equipment may also increase the usefulness of large spaces. Newer floor surfaces, replacing wood, provide a more useful base. The use of cages for golf practice, batting practice, and the like adds to variety of use. If handball walls, for example, can be folded and moved, possibly on air cushions, a large space could be outfitted for a greater variety of functions.

Another approach is the flexibility of the enclosure. The use of cable- or air-supported structures in which a large amount of floor space can be covered inexpensively opens up new vistas of physical education space (see Fig. 5-11). If this enclosure can be installed for poor weather and removed for good weather, the colder parts of the country can have activity space that is related to the open-air spaces characteristic of Florida, the Southwest, and California.

SPECIALIZED RESOURCE CENTER

As instructional programs change, space needs change. Existing classrooms can be utilized to create a specialized resource center (see Fig. 5-12). These areas contain materials such as books, audio-visual packages, and self-learning systems. Often, the resource center is manned by an aide. The name "specialized resource center" is used to differentiate this type from the more generalized resource center or, as this book deals with the words, libraries.

Resource centers can be organized around a subject: a

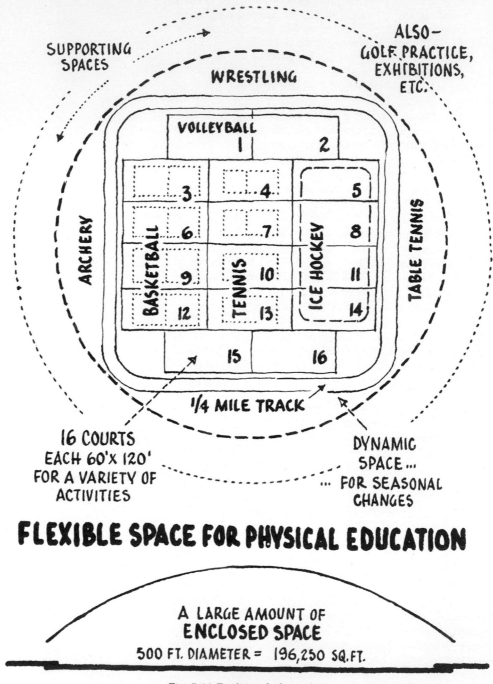

SUPPORTING SPACES

ALSO—
GOLF PRACTICE,
EXHIBITIONS,
ETC.

WRESTLING

VOLLEYBALL

1

2

ARCHERY

BASKETBALL

3

4

5

6

7

8

9

TENNIS

10

ICE HOCKEY

11

12

13

14

TABLE TENNIS

15

16

1/4 MILE TRACK

16 COURTS
EACH 60'x 120'
FOR A VARIETY OF
ACTIVITIES

DYNAMIC
SPACE...
... FOR SEASONAL
CHANGES

FLEXIBLE SPACE FOR PHYSICAL EDUCATION

A LARGE AMOUNT OF
ENCLOSED SPACE
500 FT. DIAMETER = 196,250 SQ. FT.

Fig. 5-11 Traditional physical education plants can be replaced by cable- or air-supported structures to provide a larger amount of floor space at a lower cost.

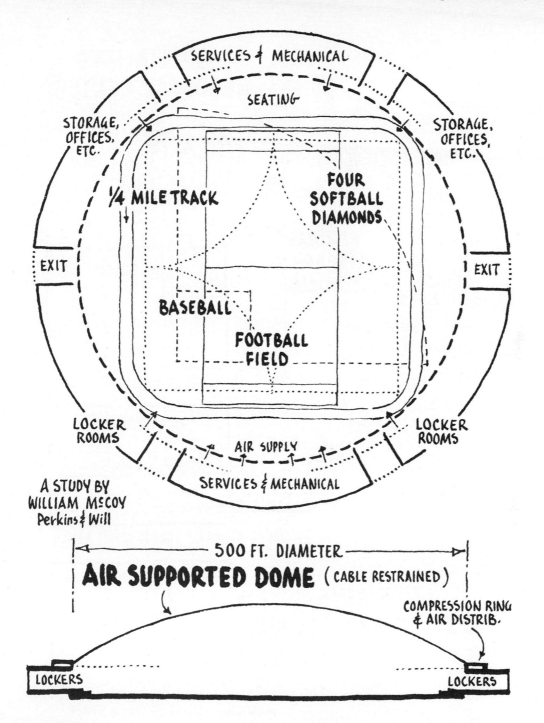

SERVICES & MECHANICAL

SEATING

STORAGE, OFFICES, ETC.

STORAGE, OFFICES, ETC.

¼ MILE TRACK

FOUR SOFTBALL DIAMONDS

EXIT

EXIT

BASEBALL

FOOTBALL FIELD

LOCKER ROOMS

LOCKER ROOMS

AIR SUPPLY

SERVICES & MECHANICAL

A STUDY BY WILLIAM McCOY Perkins & Will

500 FT. DIAMETER

AIR SUPPORTED DOME (CABLE RESTRAINED)

COMPRESSION RING & AIR DISTRIB.

LOCKERS

LOCKERS

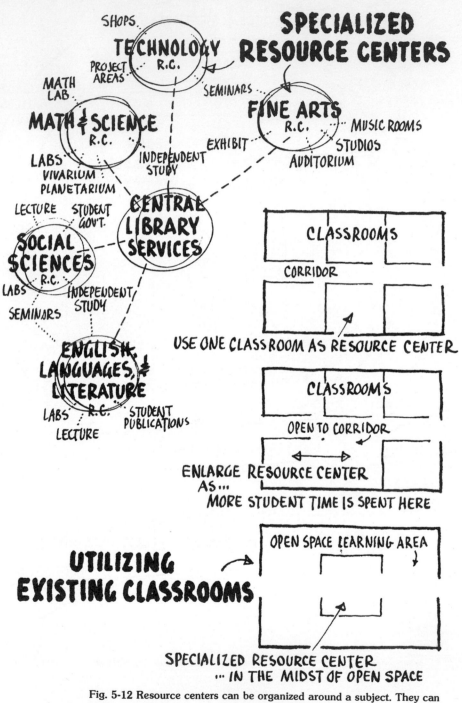

Fig. 5-12 Resource centers can be organized around a subject. They can begin in a small way and expand as utilization increases.

mathematics laboratory is a resource center. Or the center may focus on an interdisciplinary problem such as "How can man improve the quality of urban life?" The resource center can be a room or a portion of a large space. Resource centers in large spaces are sometimes called resource islands.

The usual scenario in the traditional school is to take over a room and use it for this purpose. Some of the student time formerly spent in classrooms is spent in the resource center working independently and being helped by the staff assigned to the center. As more student time is spent in the resource center and less in class groups, the need for space to house the class group diminishes and the need for resource center space increases.

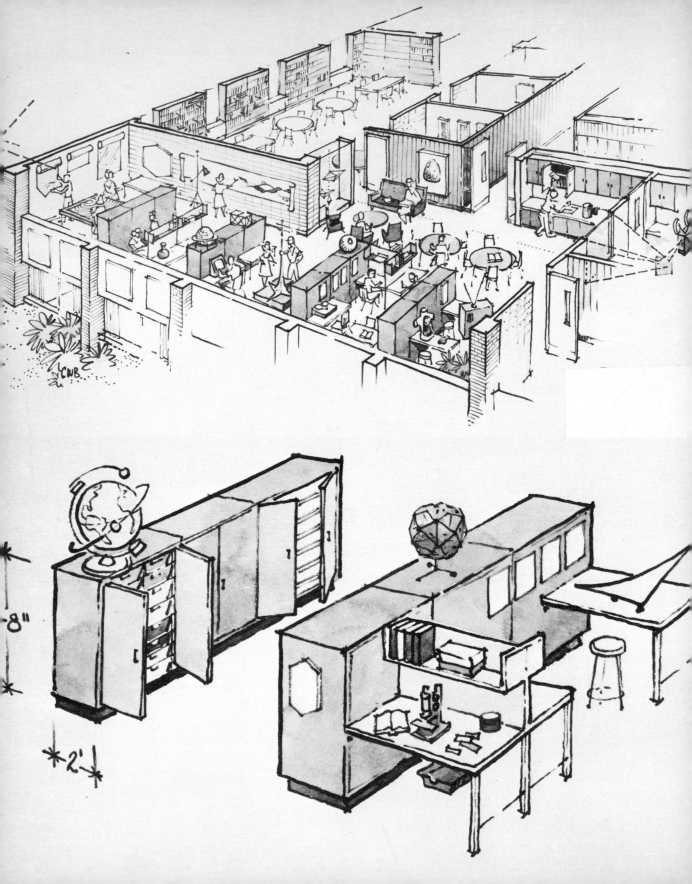

CHAPTER 6

EQUIPPING THE MIDDLE SCHOOL

■ ■ THE MOVE FROM the junior high school, where the action froze some years ago in favor of a junior school in the image of a senior high school, to a middle school that looks at children of that age remains a good move. As faculties attempt to shape spaces in response to a greater understanding of children and of the needs of the program, let us consider these factors:

1. There are astounding differences between boys and girls at this age. In addition to the obvious and cherished differences, the girls need to have a social life with older boys, while most of the boys shun girls like the plague. Perhaps there are levels in the social program that could invite in older boys and amuse the younger ones.

2. This is an age of curiosity, particularly if the school has not stamped it out: laboratories, shops, paint, growing places, clay, planetariums, TV equipment, telescopes, rockets, and on and on. There should be big spaces where all sorts of things can be used, made, and taken apart with safety and with freedom. We should nurture the curiosity, not channel it into disappearance.

3. Middle schools are made up of children who are very social animals or want to be and don't know how. The need to belong to a group because one is unsure of how to be oneself is very real. Use it. Make sure that all the students are as far into or as much a part of the group as they can be. The guidance counselor would do well to spend his or her time out of an office and in the action of the school, helping.

TOP AND BOTTOM: LEARNING LABORATORY, SKOKIE MIDDLE SCHOOL, WINNETKA, ILL.

EATING: IMPORTANCE OF MODIFYING THE EATING ENVIRONMENT

There is probably no more inhumane space in an educational institution than the usual gorge-and-go school cafeteria. Adults should be required to suffer the noise, the crowding, the food, and the lack of a pleasant ambience until something happens.

Food on wheels, in all its many forms, makes dispersed, varied, dining spaces of human scale possible, economical, and a part of the learning experience of the school. The large cafeteria must go (see Fig. 6-1).

Concessions, simple, varied food areas, self-service vending, and a variety of approaches should take the large cafeteria's place. As far as possible, students should operate the small, self-contained units, perhaps purchasing the supplies in convenience food form from a central

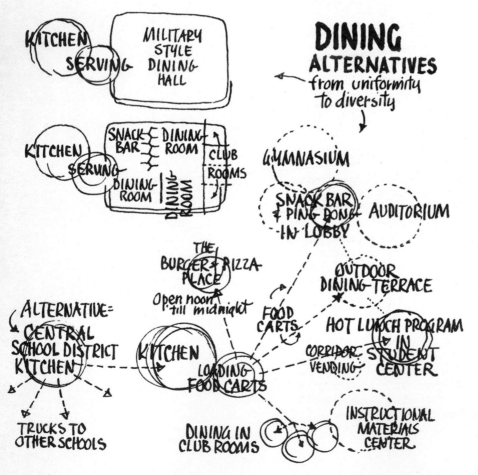

Fig. 6-1 The large cafeteria must go and be replaced by a variety of feeding areas.

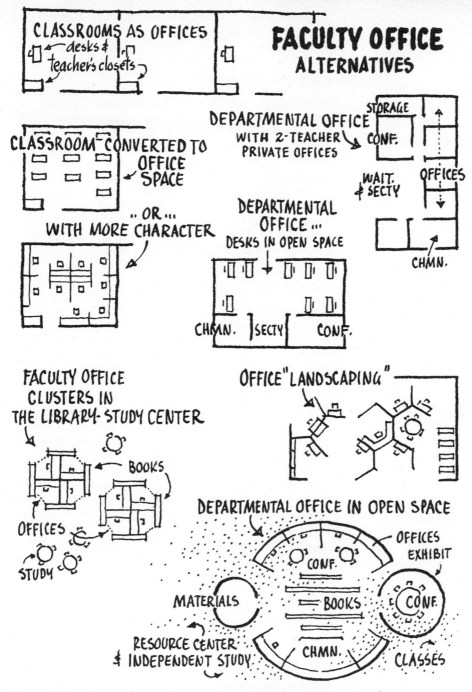

FACULTY OFFICE ALTERNATIVES

CLASSROOMS AS OFFICES
desks & teacher's closets

CLASSROOM CONVERTED TO OFFICE SPACE

.. OR ...
WITH MORE CHARACTER

DEPARTMENTAL OFFICE
WITH 2-TEACHER PRIVATE OFFICES
STORAGE
CONF.
WAIT. & SECTY
OFFICES
CHMN.

DEPARTMENTAL OFFICE ...
DESKS IN OPEN SPACE
CHMN. | SECTY | CONF.

FACULTY OFFICE CLUSTERS IN THE LIBRARY-STUDY CENTER
BOOKS
OFFICES
STUDY

OFFICE "LANDSCAPING"

DEPARTMENTAL OFFICE IN OPEN SPACE
CONF.
OFFICES EXHIBIT
MATERIALS
BOOKS
CONF.
CHMN.
RESOURCE CENTER & INDEPENDENT STUDY
CLASSES

Fig. 6-2 When planning faculty offices, make sure that they are located so that students can easily find them and feel welcome in coming to them.

kitchen and reconstituting them at the point of sale. There can be real experiences in ordering, managing, and handling money, people, stock, accounts, taxes, and the like.

FACULTY OFFICES

As schedules change, fewer faculty members have their own rooms. In consequence, alternative places for faculty to work become important. In addition, there is an increasing realization that faculty members must plan together and that such planning is a basic characteristic of any successful shift in what happens in schools.

The location of the faculty space is a strategy. If the space is behind a closed door, it is off limits to students. If it is in the midst of students, it invites consultation, informal and formal, and interruption. Perhaps teachers are in a school in order to be interrupted. See Fig. 6-2.

ADMINISTRATIVE OFFICES

Where is the new school administration located? There frequently is a manager near the entrance, handling the public, the health-attendance problem, and some discipline as well as getting the things the school needs and sending out the information the system needs.

There may be an instructional leader in the backup area. Consider the mix of resource area and the graphics, audio-visual, and print resources needed by teachers. Off this area is a professional library, the instructional leader's space, and secretarial space. Also nearby are counseling services, an aid to instruction.

Office landscaping (Fig. 6-3) is a natural, provided there are some secure places for student records and several conference rooms where people can go to pieces without embarrassing themselves before others.

Fig. 6-3 Office landscaping gives a sense of privacy but also provides a free, open environment.

CAFETERIA: A MULTIPURPOSE ROOM

	Square feet
Seating 200 for lunch (12 square feet each)	2,400
Service area (food prepared elsewhere)	400
	2,800

Suggested Equipment

- Folding portable dining table with bench; on casters; seating approximately 15 children; table height, 24 inches; bench height, 15 inches; occupying approximately 8 square feet of floor space when folded

- Mats for large-group seating; approximately 200 square feet
- Large sink for cleanup purposes; food service equipment not included

To accommodate the use of the cafeteria as a commons area it is suggested that lounge seating and chairs be provided. Upholstered benches could be used.

ART

In a humane school the arts should permeate the whole setting (see Fig. 6-4). Too frequently today, the art class shares with physical education a release from a formal, abstract environment. The art area becomes a place where restraint is difficult and games are dominant. Who controls? Who wins?

In the modifiable environment the art rooms may disappear and turn up as interest centers in the open space, as sidewalk art studios, or as one of the categories of media involved in communication. Under some circumstances the art studio could move from a one-teacher space to a multiteacher space, from enclosed to open space, at least in part, and from a centralized to a diffused role.

The art studio may become an open laboratory, to be used by students on their own demand schedule.

In a school designed around people, opportunities for the felicitous display of things of beauty will increase immeasurably. In the arts, the school may find a process from hard-line space (storage, kiln, painting area) to softer lines, to crafts, to an illustration mixture with other areas, to the outdoors, beyond lines and out in spaces.

SCIENCE

The science area can easily become a modifiable environment. The umbilical cords of science, the connections to utilities, are capable of quick connection or snap-on kinds of connections for everything: gas, water, soil line, electricity, exhaust.

The area where laboratories are to be located should contain a grid of utilities with modular locations where the connections can be made. The provisions for laboratory work should be grouped essentially around a service island and tables that can be butted against the island. The service island can be disconnected and relocated in accordance with the network of utilities.

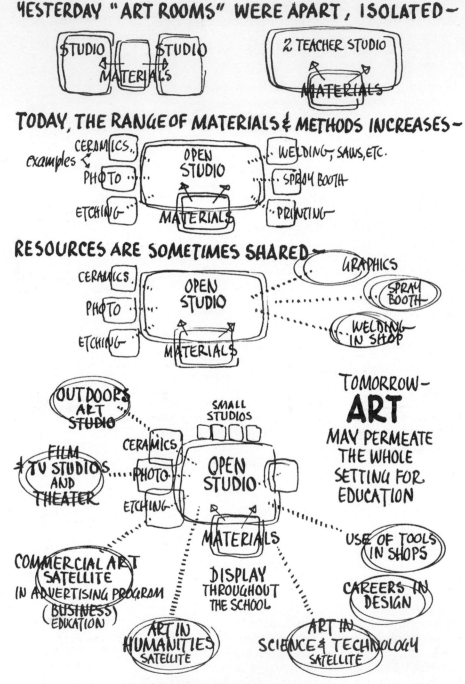

Fig. 6-4 Integration of art and education.

The laboratory can be changed from a traditional demonstration laboratory to an open laboratory in which students select their own times for work with the science equipment. A larger open laboratory allows better supervision by aides with the staff and greater utilization of the space.

The middle school is the place for this kind of equipment. The excitement and romance of a laboratory can become the most distinctive asset of any school.

SPECIAL EDUCATION

When children can learn at differing speeds that depend upon their ability rather than the preference of a teacher, there is no need to segregate most exceptional children in a special environment. The school should provide sympathetic and skilled special help for exceptional children as part of the process of individualizing learning. The student with special needs is a part of the total group of children for as much of the day as he or she can use.

STUDIOS

As more and more media are introduced and used in the learning setting, the definition of art and, hence, of the studio or workshop for art changes. Studios for television, sound recording, film making, and photography have their own specialized requirements.

To modify space so that it takes on the characteristics of a studio is not simple. Problems of lighting and the need for greater ceiling height, sound isolation, and a heavy utility load all must be considered. On the other hand, the TV tape recorder is portable, and portable darkrooms can be secured and related to the utility network. Moreover, it is possible to secure a portable piece of sound environment: a sound-isolated package or room capable of being moved.

A study of this area might determine that only a few very special environments are needed within a work space in the new media. For the most part, these can be inserted in a more general environment as permitted by the utilities network.

HEALTH SUITES

Services in this field vary widely in schools. When use of the school nurse prevails, the facilities are reminiscent of the old-time hospital approach. One wonders why schools underutilize expensive, highly trained people in the health field when nurses in the hospital setting work at a much more responsible and professional level. Perhaps the health worker to be involved in a school is the paraprofessional, with less frequent supervisory control by a registered nurse. The need for elaborate health facilities in a school would be reduced, and the space would be used for first aid and for referrals to appropriate agencies.

TOILETS

Toilets have been among the items that are not generally flexible in a school. There are two ways to deal with this problem in approaching a modifiable environment. One is to locate toilets, either in planning new construction or in modifying old construction, outside the arena. This allows change to take place in the major enclosure without interference from the plumbing.

A second approach follows the development of package toilets. Their use permits the insertion or removal of toilet rooms in toto, with only the problem of water, electricity, and waste lines remaining. The development of prefabricated bathrooms for housing may precede a similar development for institutions and office buildings.

UTILITY NETWORK

In keeping with a structural system in which interior positions are demountable or readily removable, the utility system for a modifiable environment is strategic. Lighting, lighting controls, air conditioning, and heating must be capable of being rewired or of going up partitions.

The utilities needed for living and learning, electric power, water, waste lines, telephone, retrieval and communications systems, and similar services together require a rigorous analysis and rationale. It is economically out of the question to provide all utilities everywhere. What is needed is an assignment of space to levels of utility needs, allowing a reasonable margin of safety for the usual amount of change and making possible major change beyond that point, as shown in Fig. 6-5.

SUGGESTED EQUIPMENT

The suggested goals of the middle school have enormous implications for the development of equipment and furniture lists. The equipment for a middle school should

■ Suggest a different open-ended approach.

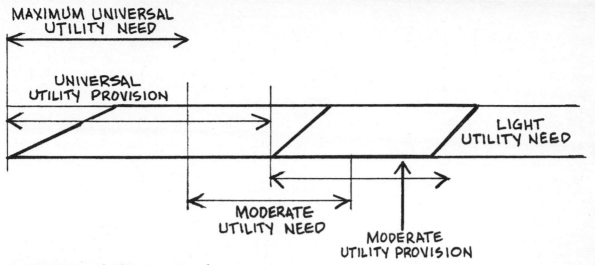

Fig. 6-5 Provision of utilities to meet needs.

- Accommodate differences in furniture arrangements.
- Be available in a variety of sizes and heights or be adjustable.
- Be easily moved and light in weight.
- Be multipurpose.
- Provide interchangeable or modular components.
- Be available in an imaginative, stimulating variety of textures and colors.
- Accommodate a variety of student-teacher uses as a work surface, for storage, as a support for educational equipment, and for the creation of easily changed boundaries.
- Accommodate a variety of student postures—lying, sitting, kneeling, and standing; seated on a seat with or without a work surface; standing on a platform.
- Be chosen while bearing in mind their use in combination with faculty contact, taking maximum account of individual student needs, interests, learning speeds, and styles.
- Keep in mind the multimedia capabilities required in every area of the school.

The furniture and equipment list in the following pages has been developed for one team group in the academic area. All the equipment mentioned is to be mobile. As much of it as possible should be modular and easily interchangeable. Work surfaces should be easily cleaned plastic surfaces. Tables and chairs should be provided in a variety of heights or be easily adjusted to accommodate the varying physical types found in a mix of grade 6 through grade 8. The use of stacking chairs would facilitate the movement of a quantity of chairs from one position to another in the cluster or from one cluster area to another. Not included in the list are audio-visual equipment, built-in counters, shelving, drinking fountains, supplies, and materials.

The aim has been to provide a wide variety of working surfaces and seating arrangements. Students and teachers or teachers' aides will be working in groups of fifty, twenty-five, ten, and five, as well as one to one and individually. To provide for all these possibilities while avoiding a fantastic clutter of chair legs, table legs, and people legs, conventional chair-desk facilities have not been suggested for every student.

The pursuit of individualization of education and independent study will result in a great mix of activities. Seminars will take place in lounge furniture groupings, at groupings of the suggested versatile platforms, in open forums, and in partially enclosed areas formed by mobile panels. Large groups or conventional class-size groups should be easily formed at will.

The funds set aside for equipment should be budgeted over the first year or so of operation. The initial purchases suggested here, which are understood to be minimal, would be evaluated by the staff in terms of quantities, quality, and function. The staff would make the additions or changes required to implement its program.

On the assumption that approximately 30 percent of the pupils will be in specialized areas (physical education, art, music, homemaking, industrial arts, theater, library resource areas, community, satellite project areas), a single interdisciplinary academic area would have to accommodate approximately 70 percent of the students at a variety of learning stations at one time. The interdisciplinary academic area would consist of a flexible teaching area that included faculty planning, consultation spaces, and science facility clusters. Space would be available for storage and preparation.

FLEXIBLE TEACHING AREA

Movable equipment needs can be subdivided into a number of basic categories: (1) work surfaces—seated-height (including tables, study carrels, work counters), standing-height, informal; (2) seating—standard, informal, specialized; (3) storage—student, materials and supplies, resource; (4) display; (5) chalkboard and tack board; (6) movable partitions (area screens); and (7) special-purpose.

SPECIFIC RECOMMENDATIONS: TYPES OF EQUIPMENT FOR OPEN SPACES

1. Work surfaces
   a. Seated-height
      (1) Plastic-surface, trapezoid tables, 30 by 30 by 30 by 60 inches; adjustable height; capable of accepting tote trays on tray support runners. It is suggested that a large percentage of the required seated-height work surfaces consist of trapezoid tables. Used singly, these tables will provide work surfaces for one or two students. When grouped, they will furnish a variety of shapes and sizes to serve small groups working on large projects, large groups in seminar, discussion, or forum situations, or requirements for a movable, continuous counter surface.
      (2) Study carrels with a plastic-work-surface desk top; approximately 23 inches deep by 36 inches wide, with varying heights. Provide a full-width shelf, and consider an undershelf light and multioutlet boxes for most carrels. Single units, rather than clusters or ganging of carrels, are suggested for flexibility of placement.
      (3) Activity carrels with a plastic-work-surface desk top; approximately 23 inches deep by 48 inches wide, with varying heights. Provide a full-width shelf, and consider an undershelf light and multioutlet boxes. Investigate special units accommodating rearview projection equipment. Flexible single units are suggested. When activity carrels are provided with a shelf light and electric outlets, they permit the use of larger audio-tutorial accessories. They may also be used for individualized activities requiring more space than ordinary carrels, such as art, two-student activities, or projects requiring many materials.
   b. Standing-height (or for use with a stool having an adjustable backrest)
      (1) Plastic-surface, oblong tables, approximately 48 inches wide by 24 inches deep by 36 inches high; used to form a continuous work counter of varying lengths. Counter units should provide room below for movable storage cabinets. Cabinets should have casters suitable for carpeted surfaces and locking brakes.

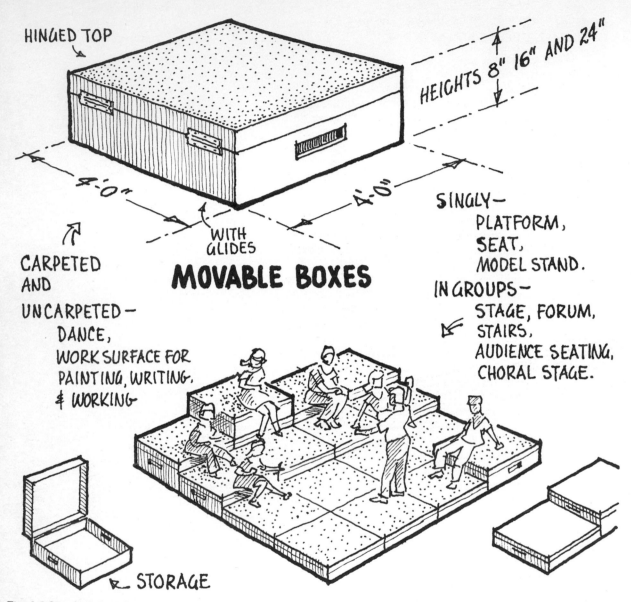

HINGED TOP

HEIGHTS 8" 16" AND 24"

4'-0"

4'-0"

WITH GLIDES

MOVABLE BOXES

CARPETED AND UNCARPETED—
DANCE,
WORK SURFACE FOR PAINTING, WRITING, & WORKING

SINGLY—
PLATFORM,
SEAT,
MODEL STAND.

IN GROUPS—
STAGE, FORUM,
STAIRS,
AUDIENCE SEATING,
CHORAL STAGE.

STORAGE

Fig. 6-6 Simple 4- by 4-foot units can be liberally dispersed throughout the school and used as work surfaces, for seating, and, in various heights, for acting and choral groups.

(2) Adjustable drawing boards
c. Informal
  (1) Floor, with tote trays having a writing surface, lap boards, and so forth.
  (2) Carpeted or smooth-surface platforms, approximately 4 feet by 4 feet by 8, 16, or 24 inches high; provided either with lockable casters suitable for a carpeted surface or with "ski" runners for sliding over carpet.

The top should be hinged or removable so that the interior may be used for storage. An alternative choice would be platforms with folding legs that could be stacked for storage. See Fig. 6-6.

2. Seating
   a. Standard: A variety of heights or adjustable heights. Consider a stacking feature and the provision of removable tablet arms for some seats.
   b. Informal
      (1) Floor cushions. Consider several varieties and shapes.
      (2) 3-seater sofa
      (3) Lounge chairs
   c. Specialized: Stools with adjustable backrests
3. Storage
   a. Student
      (1) Coat and hat storage: Mobile or wall-hung units. If mobile, use double-face units, 47 inches wide by 23 inches deep by 68 inches high, accommodating approximately 30 students each.
      (2) Tote tray personal storage, or specialized cabinets: Double-door cabinet, 47 inches wide by 23 inches deep by 68 inches high, accommodating approximately 30 tote trays; locking wheels. Tote trays are available with a hinged lid to be used as a writing surface and a handle permitting them to be carried like a briefcase.
   b. Materials and supplies
      (1) Mobile storage cases, approximately 68 inches in height, with a modular capacity to accept a variety of drawer sizes, adjustable shelves, or special-purpose trays. A double-door unit, 47 inches wide by 23 inches deep by 68 inches high, might be equipped, as one example of a possible choice of interiors, with 2 full-width shelves 30 inches apart, 4 half-width drawers 6 inches high, and 4 half-width drawers 9 inches high.
      (2) Mobile storage cases, approximately 42 inches wide by 23 inches deep by 30 inches high, to fit beneath standing-height counter tables, with a variety of drawer depths (perhaps 3 to 6 inches high with a single drawer 9 inches high, or paper storage drawers 3 inches high); locking wheels.
   c. Resource: Wheeled book carts or mobile open

shelving, 52 inches long by 24 inches wide by 42 inches high, with 4 adjustable shelves or cutouts to accommodate tote trays.

4. Display: Area screens, the backs of mobile storage units, and available wall surface are suggested initially as tack board and gallery exhibition surfaces. If the need for additional special-purpose display units, such as glass-fronted cases, becomes obvious, these items can be earmarked for future purchase.

5. Chalkboard and tack board: Available wall surfaces, area screens, and the backs of mobile storage units are suggested for this purpose. In addition, consider mobile chalkboard–projection screen–tack board units.

6. Movable partitions (area screens): An assortment of single-unit freestanding panels, preferably on wheels with locking brakes, joinable in groups of three or more. The panels should be of the type which accommodates tack board or chalkboard surfaces and from which equipment (shelves, display cabinets, work surfaces, storage units) can be hung.

   a. Freestanding curved partition, 60 inches wide by 54 inches high, with a surface suitable for attaching acoustical panels or drawing paper to create panoramas and cycloramas.

   b. Freestanding mobile panel, 48 inches wide by 54 inches high, with a mirror on one side and a tack board on the other, a chalkboard on one side and a tack board on the other, or a frame capable of accepting either mirror, tack board, or chalkboard by applying hanging panels.

   c. Joinable panels to enclose temporarily a seminar group or project area, each panel being approximately 48 inches wide by 54 inches high.

7. Special-purpose

   a. Mobile display easel, 36 by 18 by 50 inches, with removable display boards (tack board, chalkboard, felt surfaces).

   b. Open-top mobile bin, 24 by 20 inches by 22 inches high.

   c. Mobile tool counter, 50 by 18 inches, with an overall height of 48 inches; tool board above and drawers below.[1]

   d. Sewing machine with cabinet, even if separate home arts area is provided.[1]

   e. Edge-grain maple craft or art bench, suitable for hammering, 60 by 30 inches by 35 inches high, with casters, vise, and storage below.[1]
   f. Mobile planter, 36 by 18 by 12 inches.[1]
   g. Quiet module (portable soundproof unit).[1]
   h. Chair carts, if stacking chairs are provided.
   i. Mobile lectern, capable of accepting lockable tote tray below (teacher lecture station).

FACULTY PLANNING CENTERS

1. Trapezoid tables, approximately 30 by 30 by 30 by 60 inches, capable of accepting tote trays on tray support runners.

2. Adjustable posture chair with upholstered seat and back.

3. Side chair with upholstered seat and back.

4. Side files.

5. Adjustable shelving.

6. Coat rack with hat shelf above and boot rack below.

7. Cabinet that accepts 6 large lockable tote box drawers.

SCIENCE AREAS

These areas should have quick-connect-disconnect service islands with water, waste, and electric power connections. Student science tables used with these units would be provided with acid-resistant tops and tray support runners capable of accepting tote trays underneath. Tote tray storage cabinets and mobile service carts should also be provided. Science storage areas should be equipped with adjustable floor-to-ceiling shelving to accommodate glassware, apparatus, and supplies. Glassware and chemicals must be stored in separate areas. A double sink with a pegboard above is required in each science preparation area.

---

[1] Products and furnishings for future purchase after the space is occupied.

CHAPTER 7

THINKING ABOUT THE HIGH SCHOOL

■ ■ SPECIFIC EDUCATIONAL PROGRAMS and the facilities they require are presented in Chapter 3. Here we take up the general quality of living in these institutions and ways in which high schools can be modified to produce an environment that responds more fully to students as people. For the most part our suggestions are listed as questions:

1. What has happened to the space under the stairs for sitting and talking? Why are stair landings forbidding?

2. Who made the corridors straight? How would alcoves do? People like corners. Perhaps our schools are so efficient in design that they crush people.

3. When will technology address itself to outer clothing storage? The steel-lined walls that our lockers make constitute the worst possible environment for learning.

4. Can some of the space be left unfinished for students to use?

5. How can secondhand or cast-off furniture enrich a school?

6. All classes in social studies should take place in the streets of the school, under the glare of the lights, with unrelenting publicity given to the views of staff and students, thereby furthering accountability.

7. Differences in levels relate to people. Large low open spaces are for warehouses.

8. Can a drinking fountain be located so that it is not hazardous to get a drink?

9. Are the front doors used by students? Are all the other doors locked? When security is a problem, can students deal with it better than the police?

TOP: PHYSICAL EDUCATION FACILITIES, NEW TRIER TOWNSHIP HIGH—WEST, NORTHFIELD, ILL.
BOTTOM: ACADEMIC CENTER (LEFT) AND PERFORMING ARTS BUILDING (RIGHT), WHITNEY M. YOUNG, JR., HIGH SCHOOL, CHICAGO.

10. Are lobbies for basketball games only? Why not use them for students?

11. Where are outdoor student milling places that can accept students and not bother others? Where are indoor milling spaces?

12. Steps are great for sitting. Provide some inside and out as social gathering places. Outside steps should be carefully calibrated with sun and wind, right in the traffic, and with unobtrusive but evident ways to avoid the steps for those who would be obstructed by them.

13. Clubs need lounge space. Lounge space usually is for loners unless it is tied to a reasonable activity that gives an adolescent a reason to be there. Consider a ski club or a chess club. Why not locate the chess club in the action like chess club space in parks.

14. Vest-pocket parks are good in cities. Why not provide them in schools? The elements are sunlight, growing things, graphics, comfort, and young people.

15. Why is it that schools continually forget about display? Schools should be alive all over with the work of students.

16. TV, films, sound tracks, and technology are all elements of the display art. Schools will be more interesting when space and time are available for these purposes.

17. Use window seats instead of strip radiation.

18. Use openness to nature, a view to look at rather than an expanse of glass: a loving, careful setting for human beings.

19. What can we learn from the way young people sit on the floor, in corridors or anywhere we let them?

20. Are there enough meeting places, small and large, formal and informal, in a school? There should be a large number of small meeting places in every school where ten students can meet for discussions; sometimes a teacher may be invited. There can be a need for small faculty groups, parents, citizens who are concerned with the school, employees who will use the products, and so on. A good school will have enough meeting places for this kind of activity even if there are not quite enough classrooms. One good way to change a school is to equip a group of classrooms as meeting or conference rooms. It makes a difference!

See also Figs. 7-1 and 7-2.

HOME ECONOMICS

The modern home economics program has moved to include many vocational programs and is giving up the distinction between the exploratory and trade training. It accepts students who come to sew or cook as an avoca-

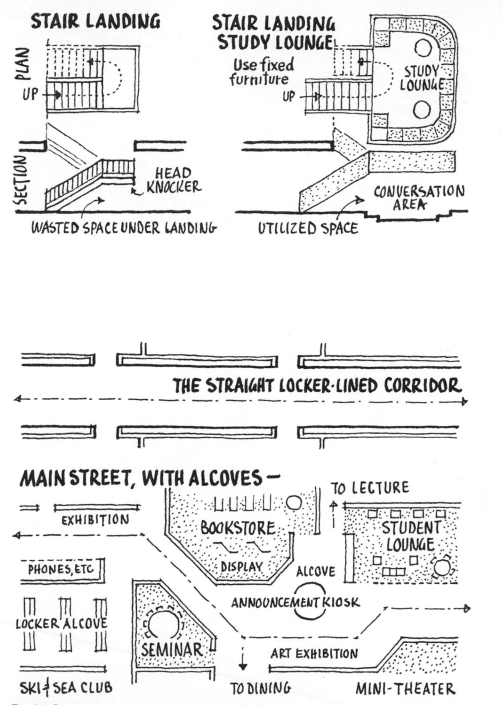

Fig. 7-1 Space under a stair landing can be put to good use (above). There are many reasons for bending corridors to give some flavor and interest to normally humdrum areas (below).

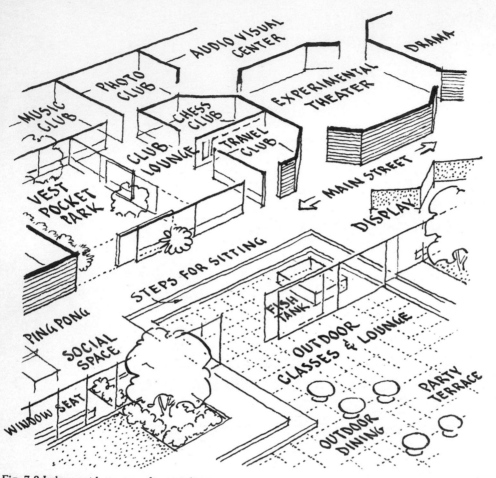

Fig. 7-2 Indoor-outdoor space for socializing and classes can be located comfortably close to indoor activity areas.

tional interest; it makes sweeping forays into family living, child care, budgeting, and consumer education; and it finds occupational spinoffs in all the programs. Space needs are further complicated by the use of the laboratories as open laboratories where students schedule themselves for work. See Fig. 7-3.

The new home economics area might include a large open laboratory in which equipment might readily be changed, for experience suggests that there are variations in demand. Sewing may be high, and foods programs low, or the reverse may be true. If we use a good component system with quick-connect utilities, we could store three unit kitchens for a while and add more work space for sewing.

Space needs that relate to vocational opportunities as well as family life programs would include a nursery school. This space should be easy to reach from exterior parking and out of the general crowding pattern of a school. Discussion areas, demonstration space, and multiuse areas also are needed.

INDUSTRIAL ARTS AS SIMULATION

Yoho's industrial arts–vocational continuum[1] is useful to think about. It follows the kind of spatial arrangement for simulation of industrial activity shown in Fig. 7-4. The simulation takes place in the open area, where a production line may be set up by a student manufacturing corporation. All aspects of technology are involved. When students need to penetrate an area in depth, they spend more time in the alcoves, become specialists, and relate to the work experience.

---

[1] Lewis W. Yoho, Dean, School of Technology, "Orchestrated Systems Approach," Indiana State University, Terre Haute, Indiana.

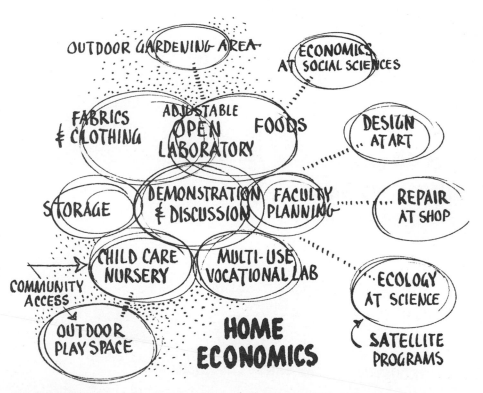

Fig. 7-3 Bubble plan of the natural evolution of a home economics area.

LIBRARY

The library, too, is changing as the names used to describe its enlarging scope illustrate. "Resource center," "learning resource center," and "instructional materials center" are among the new titles, indicating that libraries are going far beyond books as carriers of knowledge (*see* Figs. 7-5 and 7-6). The changes frequently found include the fact that libraries are:

1. Getting larger. This suggests locating the library so that it can continue to expand.

2. Adding functions, including the storage, distribution, and use of audio-visual materials.

3. Including self-learning systems. The library thus becomes a direct instruction area.

Fig. 7-4 A look at an area for industrial arts simulation where students can penetrate a topic in depth and even establish production lines in the open space.

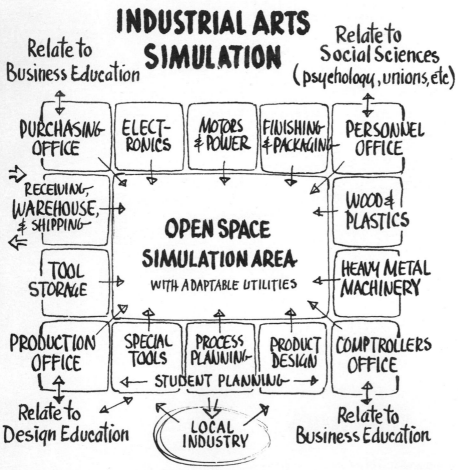

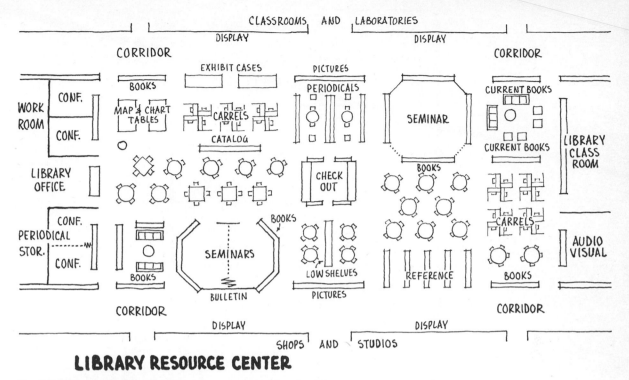

CLASSROOMS AND LABORATORIES

LIBRARY RESOURCE CENTER

Fig. 7-5 Whatever its title, the library or resource center should be planned with liberal room for expansion and with forethought given to electronic links to other centers.

4. Adding graphics, TV studios, video distribution systems, and audio distribution systems. The library becomes a production and distribution center.

5. Adding computer capabilities. Communication gets a broader interpretation.

6. Moving out of the walled enclosure:
   a. As openness in the center of open space.
   b. Everywhere on wheels.

7. Being where the action is. The new librarians love it.

8. Question-negotiation. How can the library answer the question the student does not know enough to ask, as Robert Taylor puts it.

There is a rising generation of new systems to help students find their way into the filing system of the library; these are display graphics and computer display and search systems. They will sharply change the card catalog role and that of the computer print-out shelflist.

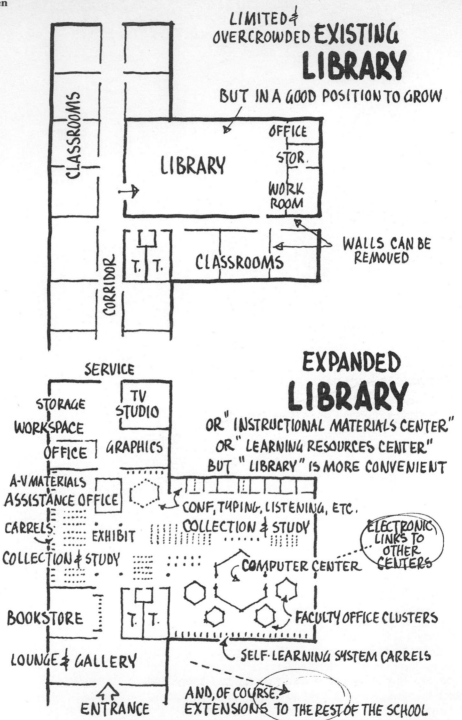

Fig. 7-6 This suggested arrangement of equipment prepared for a library resource center illustrates the informal mix of facilities that can provide a rich environmental resource.

MATHEMATICS LABORATORY

A specialized resource center, a mathematics laboratory (Fig. 7-7) is a work space for quantitative studies with aide, equipment, materials, and related facilities. The manipulation of large quantities of data is a new kind of career that access to simple data-processing equipment can support. Such use of data may involve a calculator, a programmable calculator, and a computer or a terminal and access to data-processing equipment with good-size capacity.

The use of a mathematics laboratory goes beyond a department or subject mathematics area. It could become a service center related to vocational training, business education, science laboratories, social sciences, school governance, and many other areas. The use of a laboratory to further computational skills misses the boat.

CLASSROOMS

Much of the illustration of the changes possible in open and enclosed planning relates to work now being carried

Fig. 7-7 A mathematics laboratory.

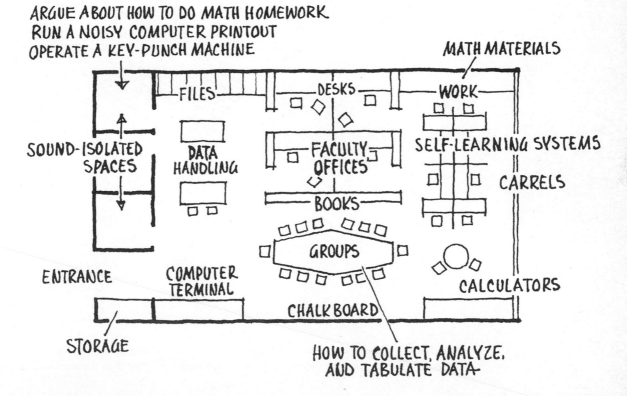

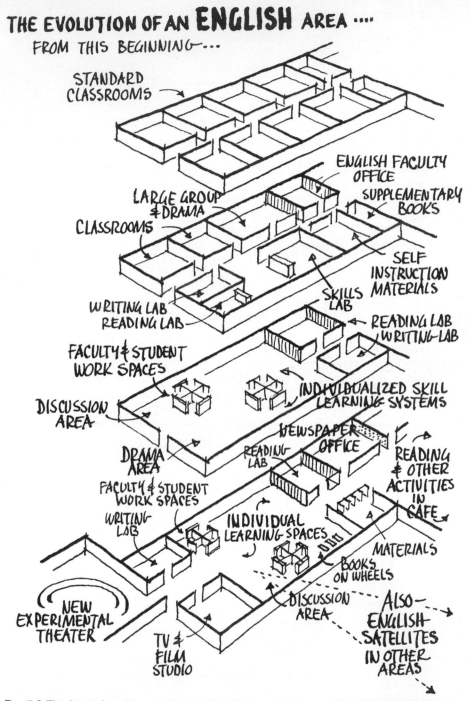

THE EVOLUTION OF AN **ENGLISH** AREA ····

FROM THIS BEGINNING ····

STANDARD CLASSROOMS

ENGLISH FACULTY OFFICE

SUPPLEMENTARY BOOKS

LARGE GROUP & DRAMA

CLASSROOMS

SELF INSTRUCTION MATERIALS

SKILLS LAB

WRITING LAB READING LAB

READING LAB WRITING LAB

FACULTY & STUDENT WORK SPACES

DISCUSSION AREA

INDIVIDUALIZED SKILL LEARNING SYSTEMS

NEWSPAPER OFFICE

DRAMA AREA

READING LAB

READING & OTHER ACTIVITIES IN CAFE

FACULTY & STUDENT WORK SPACES

WRITING LAB

INDIVIDUAL LEARNING SPACES

MATERIALS

BOOKS ON WHEELS

NEW EXPERIMENTAL THEATER

TV & FILM STUDIO

DISCUSSION AREA

ALSO— ENGLISH SATELLITES IN OTHER AREAS

Fig. 7-8 This kind of evolving chart of an English area helps the staff think through the educational program and permits the space to follow the program rather than the reverse.

TRANSITION
··· A SCENARIO

In the beginning ····

= a good orderly classroom setting
··· but with capability of change!

Then ····
··· the faculty, working together,
decides the team needs
faculty planning space,
and a seminar room.

Later ····
··· large group space is needed,
so one demountable partdion
is removed
··· and individualized learning space
is created by removing another.

Next term ····
··· the individualized program
is quite successful, so
space for it is expanded
and small group spaces are created.

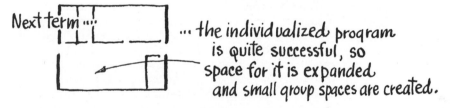

Later ····
··· the large group space is not needed,
but more small group spaces
are in demand, so changes are made
including more faculty planning space.

Finally ···
···· the faculty decides to move out
into the main space ···
··· and for materials control
a logistics center is created.

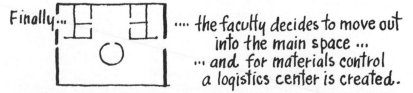

Fig. 7-9 A modifiable environment can swing back and forth as the faculty and student population changes and progresses.

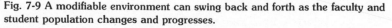

on in many schools in regular classrooms. Consider the following more specific examples:

An English classroom becomes a variety of places as drill in usage is handled by an individualized skill-learning area, deficiencies in reading are tackled in a concentrated enclosed atmosphere, things that have been read are discussed in a variety of comfortable places throughout the school, plays are played, poetry is read in a soft-drink shop atmosphere, and writing is done in the solitude of a garret. See Fig. 7-8.

Increasingly social studies is problem-oriented, whether it deals with institutions chronologically, starts with the present and goes back to roots, or conducts a kind of task force examination of what is important. Accordingly there is some tendency to eliminate redundancy in history, reduce silly requirements for state history, and substitute more of the social sciences: anthropology, economics, sociology, social psychology. These, more often than not, are considered through direct attacks upon complex present social problems. The problems of urban living suggest not so much a classroom as a study–laboratory–work space where data are collected and refined and proposals that can be subjected to rigorous discussion and analysis are developed.

The mathematics program will require spaces for individualized instructional systems as well as a mathematics laboratory and access to calculators, programmable calculators, and computers. The program will move out to satellites in quantitative terms. How does technology use mathematics? Science and mathematics are inseparable. Careful scientific use of statistical measures with reliable data is the sign of the social scientist. History is interesting; it should be studied and enjoyed, but it is not predictive. We need concentration on the tools for use by the social sciences: pure mathematics and applied mathematics. The deduction of mathematical principles from mathematics in use is a high form of the art. See also Fig. 7-9.

BUSINESS EDUCATION

The program in business education at the secondary school level continues to grow in importance as a career study area. The needs are for skill study areas, increasingly on an open-laboratory, individualized program basis, and for simulations in many forms for the use of skills under conditions approaching those of the real world. There is also a substantial use of work experience programs in the community. The enterprising business education program uses the school widely as a source of work experience. See Fig. 7-10.

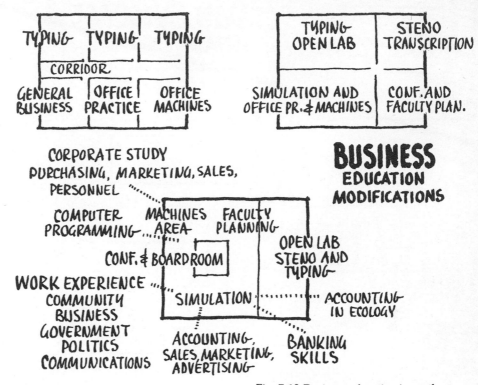

Fig. 7-10 Business education is another area that lends itself to work experience and simulation space.

FOREIGN LANGUAGE ROOMS

Foreign language classrooms have gone through the classroom-with-travel-poster stage to a language laboratory and, in some cases, to a quite highly developed, varied experience with individuals, small groups and, occasionally, large groups. Since much of the work in language requires honing of the sense of hearing, sound isolation is needed in some of the spaces.

The small enclosed area where students can work at conversation, a kind of acoustically isolated carrel where students can practice forming new sounds, a variety of listening spaces, all these are facets of the new language spaces. The need for flexibility in sound-isolated space raises real problems. There are rooms within rooms that allow one to hear normally in the midst of a steel factory. Perhaps more of these modules of quiet are needed.

The function of the language laboratory, which is still often found and frequently is well used, is being enhanced by individually operated remote retrieval systems and by cassettes with earphones and recorder-playback units.

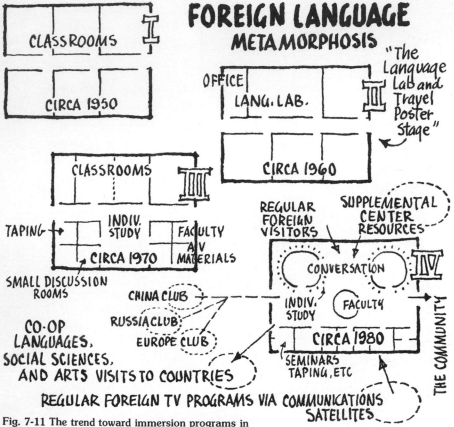

FOREIGN LANGUAGE
METAMORPHOSIS

CLASSROOMS   I

CIRCA 1950

OFFICE
LANG. LAB.   II

"The Language Lab and Travel Poster Stage"

CIRCA 1960

CLASSROOMS   III

TAPING →   INDIV. STUDY   FACULTY A/V MATERIALS

CIRCA 1970

SMALL DISCUSSION ROOMS

CO-OP LANGUAGES, SOCIAL SCIENCES, AND ARTS VISITS TO COUNTRIES

CHINA CLUB
RUSSIA CLUB
EUROPE CLUB

REGULAR FOREIGN VISITORS   SUPPLEMENTAL CENTER RESOURCES

CONVERSATION   IV

INDIV. STUDY   FACULTY

CIRCA 1980

SEMINARS TAPING, ETC

THE COMMUNITY

REGULAR FOREIGN TV PROGRAMS VIA COMMUNICATIONS SATELLITES

Fig. 7-11 The trend toward immersion programs in foreign language instruction, individualized instruction and conversation areas, and hookups with foreign television programs by means of communication satellites.

The development of immersion programs changes the game very sharply in foreign language work and could be an added reason for modifiable environments. See also Fig. 7-11.

GUIDANCE

How does a staff move from its cubicles for one-to-one guidance counseling, together with waiting space, secretary, conference room, and all the accouterments of a psychological clinic, to the current emphasis on group counseling, counseling in the midst of school, the counselor as a part of the team, informality, and guidance and counseling as triggering the response of the school to the needs of students? Despite the small size of this area, probably the greatest shifts of space are taking place here.

Counseling roles in the secondary school change as the computer takes over much of the struggle to solve conflicts in schedule. A good deal of the search to match

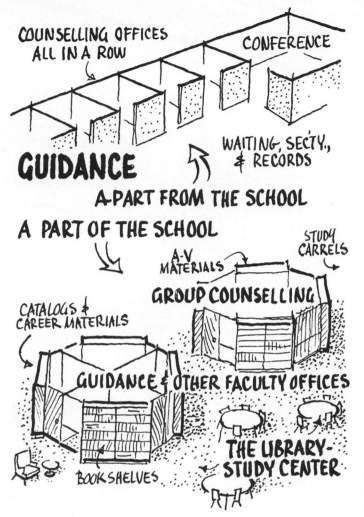

COUNSELLING OFFICES ALL IN A ROW

CONFERENCE

GUIDANCE

WAITING, SEC'TY., & RECORDS

A PART FROM THE SCHOOL

A PART OF THE SCHOOL

A-V MATERIALS

STUDY CARRELS

GROUP COUNSELLING

CATALOGS & CAREER MATERIALS

GUIDANCE & OTHER FACULTY OFFICES

BOOK SHELVES

THE LIBRARY- STUDY CENTER

Fig. 7-12 The counseling area should be comfortable and accessible rather than formal and stiff.

students with career opportunities and colleges can be done, in a preliminary way, by data-processing equipment. The need is for comfortable places for group counseling (see Fig. 7-12), for informal areas throughout the school for encounters between students and counselors, and for materials in libraries about colleges and careers with computer terminals nearby with graphic displays. There is still a need for one or two places where school staff and parents can convene, without a desk but with comfortable chairs. The guidance people need work space, record space, and someone to keep the records up to date.

CHAPTER 8

HOW TO FORECAST SCHOOL ENROLLMENTS

■ ■ COMPELLING EVIDENCE INDICATES that birth-rates and, therefore, school enrollments are decreasing. With an easing of the pressure from suffocating annual enrollment increases, everyone from board and superintendent to taxpayers to students should benefit. But before you start redirecting money earmarked for new construction, read this flat warning: Do not scuttle unpopular building programs just because the current national trend is toward lower birthrates. National and regional birthrates and enrollments provide school districts with essential background information and trends, but what makes or breaks a board and a superintendent who are projecting enrollments is hard information from their own district.

Don't be put off by the complex-sounding task of projecting enrollments or by the complex-looking tables that you may want to use to do your projecting. Plug in your data and follow the directions in this chapter, and you'll find the actual ciphering easy. Locating the raw information to be used in your projections will be the most difficult and error-prone part of your assignment.

Tables I, II, and III will help you tell the calculation story accurately for your district. Detailed directions accompany the tables. What the directions will instruct you to do is this: First, from past records find the number of births in your district for a particular year. Also from past records, calculate the ratio between births and first-grade enrollments. If families with small children have been moving away from your district or if many children attend private schools, the ratio between births in a given year and actual first-grade enrollment six years later may be

TOP: NEW NORTH COMMUNITY SCHOOL PLAYGROUND, SPRINGFIELD, MASS.
BOTTOM: DUTCHESS COMMUNITY COLLEGE, POUGHKEEPSIE, N.Y.

far less than 100 percent. If many families with small children are moving constantly into your district, the ratio could be much greater than 100 percent.

Second, figure your district's cohort survival ratio. Complicated as that may sound, it is a simple task. This ratio reflects the relationship between the number of children in one grade level in a certain year and the number of children in the next higher grade the next year. If, for example, 100 second graders were enrolled in your schools in 1968 and 120 were in the third grade in 1969 (apparently new families moved in, or there was a change in private school attendance), the cohort survival ratio between the second and third grades for 1968 and 1969 is 1.2. Calculate the cohorts between all grades for several years, determine the most consistent ratios, and, above all, be alert for trends.

Armed with the knowledge of the number of births in past years, the ratio between births and corresponding first-grade enrollments, and the cohort survival ratio, you will be able to calculate future enrollments in a pure situation. Knowing the number of births in 1972, for example, and applying the first-grade enrollment ratio to that number will yield an estimate of the number of first graders for the year 1978. Next, application of the most consistent cohort survival ratio will give the second-grade enrollment for 1979, the third-grade enrollment for 1980, and so on. When an entire enrollment projection table has been completed, your district will be able to estimate, in a pure situation, how future enrollments will shape up.

Why the twice-stated qualification "in a pure situation"? As many school people know, theories can be damaged by reality. Nevertheless, the theory should not be thrown out; it is designed to be general enough to work in many different situations. Each enrollment projectionist must crank into the general theory some practical knowledge and specific information about the district. To make your own projections as accurate as possible, watch for and avert these applecart-upsetting variables:

MAJOR CHANGES IN BUILDING PATTERNS

Patently, a district's enrollment picture is going to change if a major housing development of three- and four-bedroom units is launched within the district. On the other hand, enrollment forecasts may have to be lowered if no new housing developments are planned in a district that has been built to capacity, especially if new housing units have been fattening the district's enrollment rolls for, say, each of the last ten years.

What should you do? Create—force, if you must—

warm friendships with the municipal authorities who control zoning bestowals in your community, talk with developers before they develop. If your school district's housing patterns are changing, you may want to calculate the possible total school population when the district (or the portion of the district being developed) is filled with dwelling units. Calculations should be made in cooperation with developers or housing experts who can help estimate the expected number of children who will attend public school per dwelling unit and, if possible, by grade group.

In Berea, Ohio, the housing situation in the school district included three major separate communities. Two of the communities, Berea and Brook Park, had been sites of major housing activities in the 1960s, with 300 or 400 houses under construction each year, but the activity had dwindled to fewer than 50 housing starts in each community by 1970. Housing construction in the third community, Middleburg Heights, had picked up speed in the late 1960s and early 1970s. With opportunities for new housing units limited in both Berea and Brook Park and with a declining birthrate in both communities, it was apparent that future enrollment growth would originate from Middleburg Heights.

To understand better how the growth of Middleburg Heights would affect future enrollment, a planning group analyzed vacant land and actual and proposed zoning for the land. Then estimates were made of the number of dwelling units that could be built in Middleburg Heights and the number of children (based on the yield of similar kinds of housing already in the area) that would be brought into the district.

If school district boundaries do not coincide with community boundaries, the task of obtaining enrollment data is more difficult. New housing construction within such districts may have to be plotted by addresses on building and occupancy permits. By knowing the total number of dwelling units in a certain area and the school enrollment from that area, it is possible to calculate the number of public school children per housing unit. By watching the "children yield" per unit over a long period of time, some important population trends can be identified.

COMMUNITY PATTERNS

As children of the original families of a community grow older, school enrollments may decline. As original families are replaced, the number of school-age children may gradually rise again. Rental apartments have their own cycles, and these are related to the number of bedrooms per unit and to rental prices. If your community is new or changing, you should not neglect to note these housing trends.

NONPUBLIC SCHOOLS

Keep an eye on all nonpublic schools, especially new ones and any old ones that may be changing their enrollment patterns. The fate of parochial schools has a great impact on public school enrollments, but alternative or free or magnet schools can be a factor as well. Enrollments of many parochial schools seem to be declining, and if these schools fail to receive support in the form of tax money (the courts keep rejecting plans that would channel public money to private schools), the message to school boards should be clear: be prepared to accommodate increasing numbers of students from parochial schools.

TRANSPORTATION CHANGES

As surely as old Burma Shave signs followed old highways, new houses follow new highways. Highways and transit lines can even redirect growth patterns. If a new highway or transit line is planned to slice through your district, watch out for more cars, more houses, and more children.

INTEGRATION

When a school board must integrate its schools, another set of variables must be inserted into projection calculations. Children may have to be located geographically by grade and by race (or ethnic group). When questions of racial balance must be answered, boards should investigate enrollment patterns that could lead to certain schools becoming all black or all white.

NATIONAL TRENDS

Vance Packard calls America a nation of strangers because Americans move around so much. One major migration trend occurred when people from rural areas moved to the cities to throw their lot in with the industrial revolution. Now the descendants of those earlier migrants are leaving the cities for the suburbs. The next major migration may be back into the city, farther away from the city, or into small towns. Who knows? The point, in any case, is that what is foreseeable must be planned for by school officials. Because a great many (indeed, most) of the factors that go into enrollment projecting are eminently manageable, let's put them to work for your district in the paragraphs that follow. Complete the estimated enrollment graph (Table III), and you'll have a good idea of your district's enrollment pattern for the next decade.

CALCULATING ENROLLMENTS FOR YOUR DISTRICT

Although the table may appear confusing and the directions are long, you won't have any trouble completing Table III if you can muster some information about your own district.

The directions are given in four basic steps: (1) Find the number of births in your district for each of the past ten years (Table I). (2) Using that birth information, estimate first-grade enrollments (Table I again). (3) Using the past enrollment figures, calculate cohort survival ratios in Table II (the term "cohort survival" may be confusing, but the process is an easy one to grasp). (4) Complete Table III.

Step One

Because kindergarten enrollment figures tend to fluctuate in most districts, ignore them at first and, in their stead, use first-grade enrollments as your base to calculate

TABLE I Begin your projection project by filling in data requested on this form.

	Births	First-grade enrollment		
Year (1)	Number of resident births (2)	Year (3)	Enrollment, October 1 (4)	Ratio (col. 4 ÷ col. 2) (5)
1968		1974 ⎫		
1969		1975 ⎬ Actual		
1970		1976 ⎭		
1971		1977 ⎫		
1972		1978		
1973		1979 ⎬ Estimates		
1974		1980		
1975		1981		
1976		1982		
1977		1983		
1978		1984 ⎭		

future enrollments (and then work back to kindergarten).

First-grade enrollment estimates begin with information about the number of births in a school district. The number of births in past years often is available from local health departments, state health departments, and the National Center for Health Statistics (which publishes *Facts of Life and Death* and the *Monthly Vital Statistics Report*). Birth information from these sources usually is categorized by governmental unit.

To find the number of births in your district in each of the past ten years, use information from the governmental unit or units (county, township, municipality) that most closely coincide with the area of your school district. If birth data are not available, a canvass of pre-school-age children can be used to estimate future enrollments. Hospital birth registrations, head counts, and mail samplings also can be used to tally the number of children of preschool age, but these data should be given a wide margin for error.

Step Two

Look at Table I. Fill in the number of births (column 2) for each of the last ten years; you may have to estimate births for the most recent year or two. Go to column 4 and fill in actual enrollments (as of October 1) for the years 1968 through 1972.

Now, for a little calculating: In column 5, figure the ratio between resident births (column 2) and actual enrollments (column 4). The ratio (devised by dividing the figure in column 4 by the figure in column 2) will help you estimate enrollments in future years. Example: 100

TABLE II Fill in cohort survival ratios.

	Relationship	Ratio
First grade, Year 1,	to Kindergarten, Year 1	
First grade, Year 1,	to second grade, Year 2	
Second grade, Year 1,	to third grade, Year 2	
Third grade, Year 1,	to fourth grade, Year 2	
Fourth grade, Year 1,	to fifth grade, Year 2	
Fifth grade, Year 1,	to sixth grade, Year 2	
Sixth grade, Year 1,	to seventh grade, Year 2	
Seventh grade, Year 1,	to eighth grade, Year 2	
Eighth grade, Year 1,	to ninth grade, Year 2	
Ninth grade, Year 1,	to tenth grade, Year 2	
Tenth grade, Year 1,	to eleventh grade, Year 2	
Eleventh grade, Year 1,	to twelfth grade, Year 2	

TABLE III Fill out this form by using information you've collected by following directions in the accompanying text, and you'll know what kinds of enrollments to expect between now and 1985.

Grade	K	1	2	3	4	5	6	7	8	9	10	11	12	
Cohort survival data														
Year														Total
Actual 1972–1973														
Estimated:														
1973–1974														
1974–1975														
1975–1976														
1976–1977														
1977–1978														
1978–1979														
1979–1980														
1980–1981														
1981–1982														
1982–1983														
1983–1984														
1984–1985														

children were born in your district in 1963 and 80 children showed up for the first grade six years later in 1969. The ratio (80 divided by 100) is 0.8; it should be recorded in column 5 across from the year 1969.

Fill in the ratios (column 5) for the years 1968 through 1972. Find the most consistent ratio and put it in column 5 across from the years 1973 through 1978. Example: You find your consistent ratio to be 0.75. In 1970, 150 children were born in your district. By multiplying your ratio (0.75) by 150, you can estimate that your first-grade enrollment for 1976 will be approximately 113 children.

Complete Table I—you'll need all its figures a little later.

Step Three

Table II will help you figure cohort survival ratios. That term simply means the ratio between the number of children in one grade in a certain year and the number of children in the next higher grade the next year. Example: If 100 children attend third grade one year and 98 attend fourth grade the next year, the cohort survival rate for grade 4 is 0.98.

To demonstrate how to complete Table II, we'll use the ratio between first grade and second grade as an example. Ratios for the other grades can be determined in exactly the same way.

Example:

1. Total the first-grade enrollments for the last eight years.

2. Total the second-grade enrollments for the last eight years.

3. Divide sum 1 (second-grade enrollments) by sum 2 (first-grade enrollments). The answer will be the cohort survival ratio for grade 2.

4. Repeat the transactions in 1, 2, and 3, using enrollments for the last three (rather than eight) years.

5. If the ratios from the eight-year and three-year calculations differ greatly, try to determine why. Then decide which ratio to use, favoring the three-year calculation if no other variables are present.

Follow steps 1 through 5 for each of the twelve grades.

Complete Table II.

Step Four

You have finished all the hard work. The final step in projecting enrollments is the completion of Table III, simply a matter of plugging in data and doing some multiplication.

Across the top of Table III, fill in the cohort survival ratios for each grade (information from Table II).

Along the left side of Table III, fill in first-grade enrollments (from Table I).

Starting with 1972–1973, multiply grade 1 enrollment by the cohort survival ratio for grade 2, and post the answer in the grade 2 column on the line marked 1973–1974. Continue by multiplying the grade 2 enrollment for 1973–1974 by the cohort survival ratio of grade 3, and put the answer under grade 3 for 1974–1975.

After you've completed calculations through grade 12, you'll have figures posted in a diagonal line beginning at the upper left and sliding down in position to the lower right on Table III. To fill in the squares on Table III below this diagonal line, go back and repeat the exercises of step 4 exactly as you've done thus far but beginning this time with the grade 1 enrollment for 1973–1974. Then repeat the full grade-by-grade calculations, beginning this time with the grade 1 figures for 1974–1975, then 1975–1976, and so on to the end. With each grade-by-grade step, the work will lighten: each diagonal column of figures will have fewer squares to be filled.

The mathematics are simple. Example: Let's say that 120 children are enrolled in the first grade for 1975 (you've posted this figure on Table I). Continuing the example, let's say that the cohort survival ratio for grade 2 is 0.97 (which you have posted on Table II). Multiply 120 by 0.97, and you can estimate that 116 children will be enrolled in grade 2 in 1976.

Here are some points to remember:

Your base is grade 1. To estimate kindergarten enrollments, you'll have to work back one year. If a substantial number of first graders are retained, you may want to use the second grade as your base and work backward to the first grade and kindergarten.

Be on the lookout for the variables mentioned in this chapter. You may already know that your ninth-grade enrollment consistently shows increases over the previous year's eighth-grade enrollment because of immigration from nonpublic schools that do not provide schooling after the eighth grade. But don't forget to change the estimates if nonpublic schools close or cut back.

Use enrollment figures as of October 1 of each year (or from approximately six weeks after school begins). Enrollment figures from either of those points are more stable than first-day-of-school enrollment figures.

In completing Table III, continue to work in the diagonal (downward), because you should be comparing one year's enrollment with the enrollment in the next grade for the next year.

GLOSSARY

GLOSSARY

action office   Work office in which there is little ceremony and access to the administrator is not controlled by his or her secretary.

arena   Area that operates as a curriculum center for an in-depth study of an interdisciplinary problem.

carrel, activity   Table with high sides and back, designed to create an element of privacy for study, that contains preset elements for a study project. An example in biology might be materials and tools for a self-taught dissection, which would include filmstrip and projector showing stages in dissection; tests to be taken before students start and after they have finished a written set of directions on how to dissect the material; and an audio-tape player with a headset that takes a student, by spoken instructions, through the process step by step.

carrel, study   Semi-isolation booth in which people can study.

child care program   Program designed to care for preschool and primary school children whose parents are working. Such programs range from custodial baby-sitting to highly professional operations.

cluster   Group of activities or way of organizing separate functions around a common idea or space. Groupings of vocational skills, such as jet engine mechanics, piston engine mechanics, automobile body repair, automobile mechanics, and diesel mechanics, and small motors such as outboard, motorcycle, or snowmobile engines, can be made into a cluster related to transportation.

cohort survival ratio   Method of predicting student body size in terms of the number of students who, for example, were in first grade in the preceding year and showed up in second grade in the current year.

community   Small subdivision of a school that can operate as a unit. It is supposed to have a warm feeling.

core areas   Generally common or basic learning areas. For example, one common core of studies links English and social studies as an interrelated element going through a middle school.

course   Program of studies, usually in a single academic area such as trigonometry, United States history, or earth science. Courses are taught in a semester, year, or other time interval.

course, block-type   Program of studies in which two or more subject areas are taught in a block of time by one or more teachers (for example, United States history and American literature). Such a course may be taught in a larger time block than a single period.

creativity   Ability to reorganize elements in (to the student at least) new patterns. Sophisticated schools are learning how to help students develop this kind of talent, which is quite different from the usual academic talent.

curriculum, latent   Unspoken curriculum in contrast to that intentionally taught. It includes the basic attitudes that teachers, school, and society have about the values of school, the worth of the individual, democracy, and other people, and their feelings about minorities. Recent attention to this area has brought about a close examination of what we teach inadvertently, such as the expectation that women are passive.

curriculum, overt or manifest   Concepts, facts, and values that the staff and school state they are teaching, such as the phylogenetic tree in biology, the binomial theorem, and addition in mathematics.

demand schedule   Schedule organized by student needs and interests in contrast to the traditional schedule, which is organized around a set and relatively fixed series of courses, often on a yearly basis. The demand schedule permits great flexibility in arranging the use of time.

demountable partition   Wall that can quite readily be taken down in pieces and reassembled elsewhere.

diagnostic prescriptive teaching   Teaching based on assessing what a person has learned in an area, such as reading skills, and then prescribing a course of action for that individual to improve his or her skills and concepts. This is a highly individualized approach.

domain   Broad field of knowledge such as English or science.

elementary school   *See* SCHOOL, ELEMENTARY.

enclosed plan   Plan for physical facilities that consists of enclosed rooms. Floor-to-ceiling walls and doors are used to isolate spaces from each other.

faculty space   Usually faculty offices, work space, and team planning areas.

folding partition   Wall between two rooms that can be moved on demand to open them to each other.

formative testing   *See* TESTING, FORMATIVE.

hall   *See* HOUSE PLAN.

Head Start program   Federally supported program to give culturally disadvantaged preschool children a head start in school. These children too often enter kindergarten behind middle-class children and fall further behind as they advance through school.

high school   *See* SCHOOL, HIGH.

home care program   Day care program held in the homes of people whose children are involved.

house plan   Method of decentralizing a large school into several subsections, often called halls. A hall or house frequently has its own administrative head (house principal). This form of organization may combine the benefits of smallness with the assets of a large school.

hub   Center where the spokes come together.

immersion system   Organization of a school in which children have an in-depth experience in an interdisciplinary arena or problem area.

instructional resource center   *See* LEARNING RESOURCE CENTER.

item analysis   In testing, using the degree of success of a student on each part of a test to indicate where he or she should concentrate his or her learning.

junior high school *See* SCHOOL, JUNIOR HIGH.

language laboratory Facility that permits a student to work individually with tapes to improve language skills and fluency.

learning resource center Library with considerable printed and nonprinted materials (tapes, films, filmstrips, and so on). It may have a range of personnel such as independent study coordinators, aides, and technicians to work with students.

learning station Any place provided for a student in which he or she is expected to learn something related to the formal school program.

magnet school Alternative school that attracts students from a larger area than a neighborhood attendance zone. The attraction may be specialized in the arts, sciences, communicative arts, or other learning areas.

mastery learning Theory, proposed by Benjamin Bloom, which assumes that almost all children can learn a concept appropriate to their age but that differences are found in the speed with which the idea can be learned.

middle school *See* SCHOOL, MIDDLE.

modifiable environment Environment that can be changed, usually by rearranging walls that can readily be taken down and put in different places; also, a building with many demountable partitions.

module Subunit of time or a repeatable element of a building. Courses can also be broken into modules, or parts.

multischool School made up of a series of subschools much as a university is made up of semi-independent colleges.

notehand Simple version of shorthand, usually intended for high school students who are going on to college.

office landscaping Use of flexible, easily rearranged screens to create private work spaces for individuals as a substitute for floor-to-ceiling walls and doors to isolate workers.

open environment or open space Space characterized by the reduction or elimination of floor-to-ceiling walls. Equipment and screens are used to identify specific spaces within the total area.

open laboratory Laboratory available for student use whenever a student wishes, as opposed to the scheduled laboratory, in which the time for student use is rigidly scheduled.

open-plan school School with large amounts of open space.

open school British definition of a curriculum or educational procedure. This phrase has nothing to do with the presence or lack of flexible space but indicates a program in which the student exercises some degree of choice as to which area of interest he or she will work in at a given time.

open space *See* OPEN ENVIRONMENT.

oscillating system School system in which children alternate between basic studies and related arts and disciplines, giving a half day to each.

partition, demountable *See* DEMOUNTABLE PARTITION.

partition, folding *See* FOLDING PARTITION.

phasing Organizing a curriculum so that offerings change each year—for example, United States history this year, Western world civilization next year, and non-Western civilization the following year. This procedure enables a small school to offer a much greater range of courses than a traditional schedule that repeats every course yearly.

practicum Assignment in the field in which a student can test the ideas he or she has learned.

recycled space   Space redesigned for a new purpose.

resource center *See* LEARNING RESOURCE CENTER.

satellite project area   Space removed from the central project area that provides a similar if less concentrated function.

school, elementary   School usually extending from kindergarten through the fifth or sixth grade.

school, high   School extending from the ninth or tenth grade through the twelfth grade.

school, junior high   School usually comprising the seventh and the eighth or ninth grades.

school, middle   School extending from the fourth, fifth, or sixth grade through the eighth grade.

school care program   Provision of care for children in school outside regular school hours and for a wider, often younger range of ages. A mother could leave school-age children in such a program until she picked them up after work, and a three-year-old child could be cared for while the mother is working.

study carrel   *See* CARREL, STUDY.

subschool   Small school within a school; unit of a multischool. *See also* HOUSE PLAN.

summative testing   *See* TESTING, SUMMATIVE.

support spaces   Spaces beyond the instructional spaces that are necessary if specific functions are to be carried out in school. For example, storage, showers, towel laundry, locker rooms, and the like are support spaces for a physical education program that, for the most part, takes place in a gymnasium.

testing, formative   Test administered before a student starts on a learning task to determine what he or she does not know and where he or she should concentrate to learn the task most effectively.

testing, summative   Test administered after the learning task has been completed to determine how well the student has learned the task.

turf   Space around you that you believe is your territory. Anyone entering your turf without your permission is an intruder. Turf is defined as both psychological and physical space.

verbal learning or verbal education   Learning with respect to words that takes place in the home. Children learn to talk at home and learn much from their parents through listening, joining in conversation, being read to, beginning reading, watching parents read, and engaging in all the activities in which parents teach what symbols (words) mean and, by example, teach that using words is or is not fun. The verbal education a child acquires in the home is one of the most important prerequisites to successful school learning.

INDEX

INDEX